Praise for *Other People's Pets*

"Newman weaves tales of navigating the gig economy with moxie and animal/human wisdom with her unflinching look at a small Montana town mutating under pressure from Hollywood and Covid. If you want to find out if you have the right stuff to care for other people's pets during boom-bust mayhem, read this book."

— Kristi Hager, author of
Evelyn Cameron: Montana's Frontier Photographer

Other People's Pets

Critters, Careers, and Capitalism
in Yellowstone Country

a memoir

Chérie Newman

Other People's Pets
Critters, Careers, and Capitalism in Yellowstone Country

Copyright © 2023 by Chérie Newman

Published by

Bitterroot Mountain Publishing House LLC
P.O. Box 3508, Hayden, ID 83835

Visit our website at www.BMPHmedia.com

ISBNs:
978-1-960059-09-3 eBook
978-1-960059-10-9 Soft Cover
978-1-960059-11-6 Hard Cover

Cover design: Christa Schoenbrodt, Studio Haus
Author photo: Kate Bryan

For questions or information regarding permission for excerpts please contact Bitterroot Mountain Publishing House at Editor@BMPHmedia.com.

Library of Congress Cataloging in Publication Data

Printed in the United States of America

A shout out to my Best People:
Devin, Morgan, Tyler, Rob, Tayle, and Mya.
You give me heaps of joy. I love you!

A big halloooo to my gaggle of girlfriends, especially
Lynne, Shan, Terry, Edis, and Jill.
Your love and encouragement have
sustained me for almost forty years.
Yikes! We are oldsters now.

And to Salli, the Most Supportive Sister in the Universe.
Thanks for listening to all my stories.

Contents

Author's Note

Montana's history is packed with exploitation. Its moniker, *The Treasure State*, originally denoted the presence of Montana's precious commodities, especially gold, silver, copper, platinum, garnets, and sapphires. The official state motto is *Oro y Plata*, which means "gold and silver" in Spanish. The state is also replete with saleable timber, vast stretches of farm and ranch land, and places to recreate. Glacier National Park, Yellowstone National Park, and fifty-five state parks attract millions of visitors to Montana each year. Those visitors spend billions.

All this wealth and yet many of Montana's citizens (just over one million at last count) struggle, mightily, to earn a decent living. In 2022, per capita income in the state was $57,719, a ranking of thirty-fifth place among the fifty states. Unfortunately, that's cause for celebration. It used to be much lower. And more unfortunately still, that statistic is skewed by Gallatin County (where the town of Bozeman is the county seat), which, because of wealthy pandemic immigrants, reported nearly twice the per capita income gains as the rest of the state during 2020-21.*

The disparity began long ago, back in the 1860s—the gold rush decade—when wealthy individuals and business entities extracted Montana's valuable resources and then exported them and the profits—often destroying the environment, and sometimes people, in the process. The discovery of precious minerals wreaked devastation on the lives, cultures, and lands of native people. Their ancestors had inhabited territories inside what eventually became Montana's state boundaries for thousands of years. Those tribes, as they were named by the colonizers and as they call themselves, are:

1. Salish / Sélish
2. Pend d'Oreille / Ql'ispé
3. Kootenai / Ksanka
4. Blackfeet / Niitsitapi (Pikuni)
5. Chippewa (Ojibwe) / Annishinabe
6. Plains Cree / Ne-i-yah-wahk
7. Gros Ventre / A'aninin
8. Assiniboine / Nokado, Nakona
9. Sioux / Lakota, Dakota
10. Northern Cheyenne / Tsetsêhesêstâhase and So'taa'eo'o
11. Crow / Apsáalooke
12. Little Shell Chippewa / Annishinabe and Métis

These days, Montana's treasure is defined less by mineral content and more by lifestyle: access to outdoor recreation,

---

* https://montana.reaproject.org

small-town living, safe schools, and wide-open spaces. Once again, however, the environment is taking a beating and the economic inequality that began more than one hundred and fifty years ago continues to grow.

In my lifetime, I've witnessed Bozeman's transformation from a small college town to a small city. Lately, however, the growth has accelerated. It's been difficult to watch huge machines eviscerate fertile farmland and wildlife habitat. The rate at which pastures and wheat fields have disappeared under houses, apartment buildings, restaurants, stores, and entertainment venues has been shocking. But new people need places to live, of course, and a larger airport.

Most of Montana's silver and gold is gone now, exported, the money spent elsewhere. How, I wonder, can we protect the rest of our treasure? How can we preserve the natural beauty of this land with its trouty rivers, hiking trails, ski slopes, wildlife habitats, and big sky vistas? How can we create a quality of life that includes financial stability for humans as well as healthy ecosystems for our mammals, reptiles, amphibians, fish, birds, and native plants?

Chérie Newman, September 2023

Preface

Some of these stories happened last year and some occurred last century. To the best of my ability, I've written true accounts of events that happened during my work as a critter sitter and in all my other adventures. I took care not to exaggerate, which wasn't difficult because the truth is crazy enough. Mark Twain's phrase "Truth is stranger than fiction…" taunted me throughout this writing project.

The names of most of the dogs and cats have been changed. I used real names for my relatives and close friends. The pets' people are unnamed. To keep us all safe.

I've experienced a plethora of careers and life circumstances during my fifty years as an adult. In these pages, I frequently sacrifice my dignity and reputation as an intelligent person. All for the greater good. And for your entertainment.

Read. Enjoy. Learn from my mistakes. Cheer for my victories.

CHAPTER ONE

Patrick: Food and Fury

A stout, eight-year-old chocolate lab sits on the laundry room floor, staring at his food. His eyes are fixed on the stainless-steel bowl and its goopy contents. "What's the problem?" I ask him. "Eat your breakfast." He doesn't move, just continues to stare at the bowl.

I followed, exactly, the instructions the woman left me for rehydrating, mixing, and presenting his meal. But Patrick will not eat. The ingredients listed on the box of dehydrated powder show nutritional content fit for human consumption: chicken, potatoes, spinach, carrots, flax seed, blueberries, and spirulina. All organic and "sustainably sourced." I check the information printed on the side of the box to see if I've done something wrong. Nope. It would be pretty much impossible to do it wrong. The box tells me to add two cups of water to one scoop of powder, stir well, and then let it sit for two minutes, all of which I have done.

The page of written instructions, which Patrick's person left on the kitchen counter, also tells me to put half a cup of dry kibble on top of the wet mix. I did that. And yet, instead of eating, this dog sits rigid, staring at the bowl. I am flummoxed. But then I remember the woman telling me, during our interview, that he'd "been picky about eating lately." And so, I again check her instructions, just to be one hundred percent certain I've done everything correctly. I have.

"Come on, Patrick," I plead, pointing to the bowl. "Looks yummy!" Actually, it looks like overcooked oatmeal with the consistency of snot.

I'm supposed to be at an appointment in an hour, and an after-breakfast walk is included in my instructions. "What is the problem?" I ask, hands on hips, staring at the staring dog. Patrick doesn't move or respond in any way. He looks like a chocolate statue, rigid body, eyes unblinking and fixed on the bowl. I pull my phone out of the pocket in my black wool sweater and take a picture of him staring at the full bowl of food.

Patrick is the most solid, muscular lab I've ever seen. I think of him as a Tonka truck with teeth. And according to the woman he lives with, he loves to eat. He certainly doesn't look like he's ever missed a meal. "Okay," I tell him, shrugging, "I'm just gonna leave you to it."

I gather what I need for my appointment, set my computer bag by the front door, and then start to clean up in the kitchen. As I run water into the stainless-steel sink, waiting for it to get hot, I hear:

Woof.

What the hell?

Back in the laundry room, Patrick sits exactly as I left him: a statue dog staring at his bowl of uneaten food. He has not taken a single bite. Again, I stupidly ask, "What is the problem?" He continues to stare. I shrug again and turn away. He has food. I've done everything correctly. I can't force feed him. He'll eat when he gets hungry. I go back into the kitchen and start wiping the counters.

Woof.

Again, nothing has changed in the laundry room. Again, I walk back to the kitchen.

Woof.

"What?" I ask, arms extended palms up, standing in the laundry room doorway. I'm exasperated, frustrated, confused. And getting impatient. I take a deep breath, blow it out, and contemplate the situation while statue dog continues his vigil.

When faced with a conundrum, I often stare at it—the way Patrick is doing—while I wait for an insight. That feels like the best option now. So, we both stare at the bowl, him sitting, me standing. Seconds and minutes pass. Something soft begins to nudge the edge of my mind, fuzzy and undefinable. I know from experience that it cannot be named or hurried. I close my eyes, hold my breath, and sweep my mind clear, giving the thing room to declare itself.

The insight takes shape slowly, like a wispy wraith materializing into a solid form. But once it appears, the knowing is clear and certain: Patrick doesn't want the dry food in the same bowl as his wet food. "Okay, Patrick." I say, "Let's start over." I grab the bowl off the floor and set it on the counter. Back in the kitchen, I rummage around in cupboards and drawers until I find a small ceramic dish that doesn't look too precious. I pull it out and pour a scoop of fresh, dry food into it.

When I set the new dish on the laundry room floor, Patrick immediately stands up, drops his face, and crunches through the dry food with great enthusiasm. *Yay!* I take another photo of him while he eats. When the dish is empty, he turns to look at me, waiting for his second course.

Carefully, I remove every chunk of dry food from the top of the wet food in the original bowl, and add another splash of water. Patrick dances in place while I stir, his black toenails clicking lightly on the gray tiles. Before the bottom of the bowl touches the floor, he leans in to slurp at the goo with his long, pink tongue.

"Okay then. Bon Appetit!"

Back in the kitchen, I squeeze a drop of lavender and basil scented dish soap onto a yellow sponge and swipe it around the inside of a cup. I clean my breakfast dishes and wipe the counters.

Woof.

FFS!

Patrick is again staring at his food bowl, which is nearly empty, except for a few pieces of rehydrated food stuck to the bottom and sides—orange bits that might be carrots and some chunks of brown glutinous who-knows-what stuff. I contemplate this new puzzle for a few seconds. And then I remember the woman telling me, "He likes his food wet." I always listen carefully when people casually mention their pet's habits and quirks, because it's usually important information.

Alrighty then! I carry the bowl to the sink, splash in more water, and swish it around with the remaining chunks of food. Now it looks like I'm about to serve Patrick a bowl of soupy vomit. But it works. He slurps it all up. By the time I carry both empty bowls to the sink, he is a happy, happy dog, prancing, eager for his morning walk.

Before we leave the condo, I attach three photos to a text message: the one of Patrick staring at his full bowl of wet food with the dry food on top; one of him eating dry food from the small bowl; and a picture of both empty bowls. I type, *Patrick will eat the dry food, gobbles it up in fact, if it's in a different bowl!* and attach a smiling dog face emoji.

She replies: *That's so funny!! So resourceful of you. Thanks!*

I really hope the next two weeks with Patrick are easy. I need easy. The Keep Notes app on my phone has a long To-Do list waiting for my attention. I have several episodes to edit for my only podcast client who managed to stay in production during the pandemic shutdown.

But first, a walk.

■ ■ ■

Patrick wears two collars when he leaves the condo. One is his normal nylon collar, from which hangs his city license tag and a metal disc with the woman's phone number engraved on it. The other collar is a circle of metal prongs. During our first meeting, the woman showed me how to put this contraption around his neck and link it together.

"You just slip these two pointy pieces into these two end links," she said, holding up the circle of silver metal. "Just like this." She quickly straddled the lab's broad brown back and clicked the pieces together. Since she's the size of a small yoga instructor, it was easy for her to bend down and accomplish that task. Since I'm the size of a small pro basketball player, crouching over a dog is not that easy for me, especially given the amount of time it takes me to wrestle those tricky bits of metal into place. Last night, Patrick waited patiently while I struggled for several minutes to connect the two ends while the prongs pressed into his neck.

The prongs are the whole point, pardon the pun, of this collar. If he pulls against the leash, they will push into his neck, into his trachea so he can't breathe. I've never used a choke collar like this, but whenever I see dogs wearing them, I wonder what they've done to deserve such a torture device. Patrick's metal collar is a tight fit, and it takes me several tries to get it on him. I wish I could simply clip his leash to his nylon collar, but that's not an option. According to my instructions, he is not allowed outside the condo unless he's wearing the choke collar. Not even in the hallway.

The condo is on the fourth floor of a building in downtown Bozeman, one block north of Main Street. There's no fenced yard. No yard at all. I wonder about the mental health of a Labrador retriever confined to a hotel-like building surrounded by concrete and asphalt. He's been here for about a year. If all goes as planned with architects and contractors, however, he'll live in a residential neighborhood within six months. A year and a half in a seven-hundred-fifty-square-foot space must seem like forever to a lab.

When I throw a toy for Patrick, he can only run about four feet before crashing into a wall or a piece of furniture. There's a short hallway, but it's occupied by a bench, a dresser, and a row of the woman's footwear. The condo is tidy, but it's full of furniture and other things. Last night, after a few throws, Patrick refused to bring his rubber bone back to me. Instead, he flopped down on the floor and began to gnaw on it. Because, really, what's the point of trying to run in such a small space? So frustrating. But he seems resigned to his situation, accepting what is. I could learn a few things from Patrick.

I just hope he's not depressed. His energy seems low for a retriever. Retrievers were originally bred as hunting and sporting dogs, first in the wide-open spaces of the Labrador region of Newfoundland, Canada, and later in Britain. They love to run and chase things, to be active and play with other dogs. Labs are famously friendly, a trait that, according to the American Kennel Club, makes them "America's most popular breed."

To get outside, we ride the elevator from the fourth floor to the ground level and then walk through a lobby and down a wide hallway toward a wall of glass that includes the back entrance door. There's an alley at the back of the condo building. Between the building and the alley is a narrow strip of landscaping—a row of short bushes and clumps of grasses with just enough space and foliage for a dog to sniff and pee after the sun goes down. Thank goodness. Last night I wasn't eager to walk the intermittently icy sidewalks in the dark, especially not with an unfamiliar dog who needs to wear a metal choke collar.

Patrick's schedule includes going outside four times each day. He gets a long walk in the morning, a short one at noon, another long walk in the late afternoon, and a quick visit to the bushes in the alley just before bed.

So, after my glorious triumph of getting him to eat breakfast, I put the spikey collar around Patrick's neck, which isn't any easier the second time, and clip the leash to it. We ride the elevator downstairs and walk along the alley, aiming for a sidewalk on the nearest residential street. It's cloudy, windy, and cold. I'm glad I grabbed my warmest coat and a pair of wool mittens before I left home yesterday. Patrick sniffs all the bushes along the alleyway. He marks his territory with a few quick squirts of pee, saving most of it for later. He walks slowly, examining low branches and rocks while I stand and wait for him to move forward again. Despite the cold wind, it feels good to be outside, to breathe in clean air instead of the stale stuff recirculated through vents in the condo building. I close my eyes and tilt my face toward the sun, even though it's mostly hidden by gray clouds. My imagination fills in the warmth. Patrick moves forward. I open my eyes and follow him down the alleyway along a row of lilac bushes that end at Willson Avenue.

We're just about to pass the last of the bushes and turn onto the sidewalk when a sweet-faced Golden Retriever suddenly appears, walking next to a tall man in a black jacket. Patrick goes from zero to ferocious in a split second. With amazing speed and force, he emits a menacing growl and leaps toward the other dog. The leash goes taut as my arm is yanked forward. Hard. It takes all my strength and body weight against the leash to keep him from lunging at the other dog's throat. The guy with the Golden shouts at me. I shout at Patrick and yank him backward. People stare. Drivers slow their vehicles to gawk.

By the time I've managed to drag him away from the other dog and backward into the alley, I'm panting, and Patrick is coughing, his trachea severely compressed by the choke collar. He shakes his head, chuffing and stepping in a sideways circle. I should loosen the collar and make sure he's okay. But right now, I don't care about him. A bright blaze of pain runs through my right shoulder. I lean over, hands on knees, gasping.

When I can almost breathe normally again, we walk quickly back down the alley and over to the patio area behind the condo building. I sit on one of the concrete benches near the back entrance—to recover and sort through my racing thoughts.

During our interview, Patrick's person said, "He can get a little aggressive with other dogs."

A little aggressive? Like he growls a little, or like he *attacks* other dogs a little? I should have asked her for details. Sometimes, in the moment, questions that should be asked don't occur to me. I was busy making friends with Patrick while I admired the beautiful green and gold quilt draped across one end of her couch. Creating a connection with pets is what I focus most on during interviews. Because, when people see that connection, they hire me. I can always ask questions later, but—to loosely paraphrase Will Rogers—I only have one chance to make a good first impression. People are impressed when their pets like me. In this case, however, I regret my lack of curiosity about the need for a metal collar.

The concrete bench is cold. The air is cold. I pull the hood of my gray puffer jacket over my head and look down at the paving stones, waiting for my heart to stop thudding against my ribs. Oh my god, I think, if I have a heart attack right now, no one will know who to call when they find me dead on this bench! I don't have any identification with me—only my double-password-face-recognition-protected phone. My daughter doesn't know where I am. I need to send her the address and Patrick's person's phone number right away. But wait. What if I have the heart attack later when I'm inside the condo? I should have bought a smart watch in the Verizon store last week.

But my daughter won't be able get into the building even if she knows where I am, because only residents have a key card for the elevator, and there's no attendant in the lobby. And how would emergency responders get to the fourth floor? I haven't seen a phone number posted anywhere on the ground floor that a non-resident could call. There are two restaurants and a coffee shop there, but no server in any of those places would know who to call about getting access to residential floors. I could die up there! Patrick will eat my body and shit all over the floor before his person returns from her trip and finds the mess. Or would he bark constantly until another resident contacted the building manager? Is there a building manager?

Without a command or invitation, Patrick sits next to me, oozing an unfamiliar friendly charm. He is now an exemplary Labrador Retriever—a shining example of the labs described on the American Kennel Club and breeder websites: friendly and affectionate. He licks my hand, leans against my leg, and lays his head on my knee. I can't tell if he's acting like nothing happened or apologizing. Whatever. He soon gets distracted by birds flitting from branch to branch on the leafless trees in the back yard across the alley and stands up to sniff the air. Within three minutes, he's gone from calm to ferocious to (possibly) contrite and back to calm—as if nothing happened between calm and calm. Once again, I think about life lessons I could learn from Patrick.

When my heart rate finally slows, we set off in the opposite direction from where we encountered the Golden. At the other end of the alley, there's nothing to block my view of the sidewalk running along North Tracy Avenue and into the residential neighborhood. I visually scan the area, searching for dogs. As we walk, I continue scanning and move to the other side of the street every time I see another dog. We make it to the neighborhood park, several blocks away, without an encounter.

While Patrick carefully smells each piece of playground equipment, I constantly check the area, monitoring our proximity to other dogs. If they get too close, I pull him away.

We leave the park when a black lab arrives to chase after a lime-green ball thrown by a young man wearing a Montana State University hoodie. The ball sails through the air and lands a few yards away from where we're standing. The dog sprints toward it, and us. Patrick growls. I yank him out into the street. He coughs as the metal prongs press into his neck, but I don't stop to let him recover until we're across the street and halfway down the block.

We walk back to the condo building on a zigzag-y route as I maneuver us as far away from all dogs and people as possible. If a sweet, middle-aged Golden Retriever provokes such fury in Patrick, I don't want to risk any other encounters.

Scanning, maneuvering, zigzagging, and avoiding becomes my strategy. Patrick, of course, enjoys our walks immensely. The more zig-zag-y the better, in fact. But for me, each outing is filled with tension and anxiety. Even getting out of the building is difficult.

The next morning, as we stand in the hallway waiting for the elevator, the door slides open to reveal a woman and a small white poodle. Patrick instantly morphs into killer dog, lunging and growling and barking. The woman shrieks. The poodle yips and cowers behind her leg. I drag Patrick across the wide hallway and over to the door that opens into the stairway, dropping "sorry, sorry, sorry" behind me as we go. I shove him onto the landing and close the heavy metal door behind us. Again, I lean over, hands on knees, gasping. He stands, looking down the stairs, patient and calm, waiting, unremorseful.

We hike down four flights of stairs to get to the ground floor, where I push the door open just a few inches to check for dogs in the hallway before we step out. After our walk through the neighborhood, we climb the stairs to get back to the fourth-floor. Again, I check before we step out into the hallway. And then we run to the condo's door.

From then on, we take the stairs. I'm anxious and tensed for conflict during each moment we're in the hallways, on the stairs, and during each moment we're outside. But inside the condo, Patrick is easy to be with. He eats, sleeps, and chases his rubber bone exactly three times across the small living room before flopping onto the floor for a long session of enthusiastic chewing. Inside the condo, he seems perfectly content. Nothing about his behavior indicates that he misses his person or is unhappy with anything—once we got the food situation sorted, anyway. He accepts the difference between her and me with good cheer. This lab is not needy, but he enjoys affection—as long as it's his idea. Once or twice a day, he comes over, sits next to me, and leans in.

"Why are you such a weirdo?" I ask now, raking my fingers across his favorite neck and chest areas. Patrick heaves a blissful sigh and relaxes against my thigh.

I sort through my knowledge base about canine aggression. Most is territorial, related to dominance of property, people, or possessions: yard and home, child, food, toys, etcetera. But I don't think that's what's going on with Patrick. I believe his behavior might be triggered by fear. Perhaps there's an issue with his eyesight. Maybe the Golden retriever startled him when it appeared from behind the bush. I decide to keep that idea in mind during the next few days. Although I'm not about to let him get close to the dogs we meet in the neighborhood, I love a good puzzle and the Golden encounter might hold a clue.

I'll have plenty of opportunities to test my theory because Patrick's person has given me deposits to hold several more dates, including Thanksgiving week, which is nearly nine months away.

CHAPTER TWO

In the Beginning

I started taking care of other people's pets for the same reason most people have side hustles: extra money.

Back in the 1990s, critter sitting income helped me launch my singer/songwriter career and produce my first album. In the early 2000s, it supplemented my income during a four-year-long search for a full-time job during the financial crisis created by the subprime mortgage debacle. In 2017, after I left my job as a producer for an NPR-affiliate radio station, pet sitting-money gave me time to re-group and start a freelance audio production business.

But then, a pandemic changed the world.

My audio production business took a huge hit at the beginning of the pandemic. Most of my work at the time came from podcasters who recorded interviews at live events, then sent those recordings to me to edit. When the world shut down, live events were cancelled. No recordings, no work, no money. One of my clients quickly adapted to Zoom interviews, but a single client does not pay the bills. And so, when I received a text message from Dana, a local critter sitter, it seemed like a good opportunity. Maybe even a gift from the universe.

Dana had way more clients than she could handle. Thousands of people—pandemic refugees—had recently moved to Bozeman and the other small towns scattered around Southwest Montana. More thousands had moved here, or bought second (or third, or fourth, or fifth) homes, under the influence of the popular Paramount television series *Yellowstone*. Kevin Costner in a cowboy hat, Montana's stunning scenery shown in high definition on eighty-five-inch screens, and the fearsome pandemic all combined to create a perfect storm that prompted a sudden population surge in Bozeman.

Many of our newest residents had pets. Or they had adopted pets after they arrived, part of their new lifestyle in Montana's wide-open spaces—a romantic image of the family dog running free paired with romantic notions about living in the mythical Wild West. Also, many of the locals had adopted pets during the early days of the pandemic. They wanted a dog or a cat to keep them company while they were isolated or working from home. But eventually vaccines happened. All the people with pets began to plan vacations, weddings, and family reunions. Some returned to on-site work. Work-related travel resumed.

Local critter sitters, including Dana, were quickly overwhelmed with requests for dog walking and home-stay services.

Affluent pet owners tried Rover.com and college students. Now they wanted someone experienced, responsible, and mature. I had experience. I was responsible and well-seasoned. Mature by every definition of the word.

Dana and her clients needed help. I needed more money. Win, win! Right?

Uhm…well. Maybe.

These new clients paid two or three times more than I'd previously earned as a critter sitter. Yay for that. Demand was high, with no foreseeable end to opportunities to take on new clients. However, I soon discovered that more money came with more stressful, often unreasonable, conditions and expectations. I felt wobbly as I tried to navigate Bozeman's new socioeconomic landscape.

This place I wanted to think of as my hometown had changed. A lot. The behavior of these particular people and their pets wasn't what I was used to. At all. After a few weeks, I wondered if I could live here anymore. I also began to doubt my ability to manage the emotional and physical instability endemic to critter sitter work.

Instability has stalked me throughout my life. Would I now willingly invite it in as an everyday, perpetual guest?

CHAPTER THREE

Patrick and The Dog Whisperer

There are white tufts of polyester scattered across the antique area rug. It looks like the ceiling formed a storm cloud and snowed on the floor. While I was busy editing a podcast on my laptop at the kitchen counter, Patrick was busy with his own freelance work: pulling the stuffing out of a fuzzy pink and yellow ball—a cuddle toy his person meant as a gift for her friend's baby. I must have ignored him for too long while I worked, and now cleaning up this mess is my penance. It's hard to imagine how all that white stuff ever fit inside a small child's toy.

This is my third stay with Patrick, but the first in his new place. Now that he's living in an actual house, he seems much more energetic. He drops his rubber bone or chew toys at my feet several times a day, begging me to play with him. But even though we're not in the condo anymore, he still can't go outside unless he's trussed up in the metal choke collar and on a leash. The yard isn't fenced.

Patrick's house, located in the historic district of downtown Bozeman, has beautiful, freshly refinished wood floors throughout. The wood is soft, and his toenails leave scratches whenever he launches himself after a toy. Most of the inside remodeling work is done, but there are boxes full of the woman's stuff, as well as equipment, furniture, and other obstacles, stacked in the living room. The only clear pathway for throwing or running is in the front entryway.

Patrick and his person have only lived here for a couple of weeks. In fact, I had to bring sheets from home to put on the bed in the guest room because the woman couldn't find the box with her sheets in it. A small crew of men walk in and out of the house and the yard several times a day, doing finish work and landscaping projects. From the looks of things, the fence around the yard's perimeter won't be finished anytime soon.

So, when Patrick goes outside, I must also go outside. It's the same routine as in the condo—choke collar, leash, poop bags—but without the stairs. Patrick loves exploring this neighborhood, and he wants more time outside. Who could blame him after nearly two years in a condo? (The six-month estimated completion time had turned out to be eleven months of actual time. Building contractors in Bozeman have way more work than they can handle, building new places for people to live in the Gallatin Valley and in the Big Sky area. They're working frantically to keep up with demand. And failing.)

When Patrick's been inside too long—according to his unfathomable time clock—he sits next to me and does his statue-dog-stare thing, eyes drilling into me. He also makes odd little sounds that aren't barking or whining, but something in between. *Rrrrrhuh. Eerrrr-um. Mmm-uff. Uh-ff-uh-ff.* Whenever he does this, I know his chatter has nothing to do with bodily eliminations. He's just antsy. He wants to be outside. I have oodles of empathy for him. I felt the same way nearly every day between kindergarten and the end of high school—a desperate need to escape, to experience something new and exciting, all of which (in my imagination, anyway) existed outside the tedium of school classrooms. Now that I think of it, those antsy feelings have continued well into my adult years, making traditional employment difficult. For me, being trapped inside a building was, and sometimes still is, nearly unbearable—like spikey little insects are crawling over and under my skin. At least I can change my circumstances. Patrick is at the mercy of humans.

After hearing his weird dog-talk for a couple of days, in between scheduled walks, I decide to take Patrick for a playdate with my friend Shan's Labradoodle, Grace—a continuation of the small experiments I've been doing to discover the source of his hostility toward other dogs. It's a risk, given my experience with him, to let him near another dog. But I simply can't imagine any dog attacking Grace. She's one of the sweetest, most likeable creatures I've ever been around. But then again, the Golden retriever that Patrick tried to attack in the alley outside the condo might have been sweet and likeable, too.

The memory of that encounter makes me briefly reconsider, but I stick with my decision. Shan's expecting us. And I want Patrick to be able to run and play off leash. I can *feel* his yearning to be free—or I think I do. Maybe I'm projecting my childhood longings onto a dog? Sometimes I wonder about myself. But I'll think about that later.

I fasten Patrick's metal collar around his neck, which is easy for me now. Outside, I spread old towels on the backseat of my vehicle and tell Patrick to jump in. He leaps up and inside with surprising speed and seems excited about what'll happen next. During the drive to Shan's house, I fight off the remnants of my apprehension. I remind myself that this will be a carefully controlled experiment. If Patrick growls and lunges toward Grace, we'll be out of there lickety-split. His ferocious behavior with the Golden still baffles me, but I have a plan. I'm also curious to see what will happen with a different dog in different circumstances.

When we roll into Shan's driveway, Grace is already in the yard. She runs over to the gate and leaps for joy. She always leaps for joy when she sees a friend—me and other people she likes. Grace is a huge Labradoodle with powerful hind legs. At the height of her jumps, it looks like her hind feet are only a few inches from the top of the gate. If she were a different sort of dog, one with mischief in her heart, she could probably jump the fence. But she has never done that. I love her enthusiasm. It feels nice to be greeted with such joy.

"What do you think?" Shan says as she walks across the driveway and stops near the open window of my small SUV.

I turn to look at Patrick. It's a warm day and all the windows are open. He leans out, sniffing the air between him and Grace, reading the situation, piecing together the story of this yard and this dog through the scent molecules that enter his nose. "I think he's eager to meet Grace," I say.

Patrick isn't growling, which is encouraging. I get out and walk around to his window. I step between him and his view of Grace to get his attention. I lean in until my eyes are two inches from his. He moves his head to one side, trying to look around me. With one hand, I turn his head back toward me and point a finger on the other hand toward his face and wag it, like an old schoolmarm.

"Patrick, you be a good boy," I say, firmly. "No barking or biting. Grace is a nice dog. You be nice to her." His muscular body trembles as he stands on the backseat, alert and impatient, tail whipping from side to side. His lips are slightly curled, an expression I haven't seen on him before. Is he smiling? I step aside and watch him watching Grace, who continues leaping, eager to receive her visitors. Patrick doesn't bark or lunge against the car door. He just stands, twitching with anticipation. So far, so good.

I open the door, blocking his exit with my body until I get the leash clipped onto the choke collar. After Patrick jumps down onto the driveway, he begins to prance, his toenails clicking against the asphalt. He's impatient to get over to Grace, but I hold him back. We walk, slowly, toward the gate while I monitor his responses to her. He pulls against the leash and then stops to hack and cough when the prongs of the metal collar press into his throat. But his tail is still wagging. In fact, his entire body is wagging. I think this might work out okay. Meanwhile, Grace continues leaping, overjoyed about this potential playmate.

When we're a foot from the fence, I let out enough slack in Patrick's leash for him to move forward and touch noses with Grace through the thick welded wire grid stretched across the wooden frame of the gate. "What do you think? I ask him. He starts doing *his* version of leaping: He lifts his body upward so his front feet come about one inch off the ground while his butt and shoulders shimmy and shake. He definitely seems excited about the possibility of playing with Grace. Or at least I hope this is Patrick's version of excited, happy behavior, and not I-wanna-get-in-there-and-tear-you-to-shreds excited behavior. He's never behaved like this around me, but he looks delighted. And, yes, I think he's smiling.

"Okay then," I say, leaning down to unclip his leash. "In you go." I lift the latch and open the gate. Patrick scampers into the yard. I step in behind him, keeping my eyes on the dogs while I reach back to fasten the gate latch.

Patrick sniffs Grace in all the usual places. Grace sniffs Patrick. They do a little circle dance around each other. And then, they take off running across the grass and around the ash tree. They race back and forth across and around the yard. Patrick stops quickly to pee on the tree, to claim this new territory as his own, to leave a "Patrick Was Here" sign for the next dog that enters this yard. And then they run and run. And run and run some more in a joyful display of canine exuberance. Success!

I pull out my phone, take a few pictures, and attach them to a text message to Patrick's person: *Patrick and his new doodle friend, Grace. A successful playdate!*

I experience a moment of panic after I press *send*. I didn't ask her permission to do social experiments on her dog. But it turns out I didn't need to worry.

She responds with enthusiasm: *Wonderful to see Patrick making friends!*

■ ■ ■

Two weeks later, I'm thirty-five miles from Bozeman, walking along a dirt path that follows the low bank of land above the confluence of the Missouri River. Mid-afternoon sun sparkles on the wide stretch of water where three rivers—the Gallatin, the Jefferson, and the Madison—mingle and flow east to join the Mighty Mississippi. I'm always amazed that the Missouri River—a major character in the story of Lewis and Clark and the Corps of Discovery—begins so quietly. The first time I came out here, when I was twenty-five years old, I expected to see roiling waves and hear hydraulic collisions. But no. The three rivers simply braid together unobtrusively as they move around islands of gravel and willow thickets until they are forced into one channel by the surrounding topography.

Despite the lack of drama, however, I come here several times a year, either to walk or ride my bike. I like to watch birds and insects interact with the water. On a weekday afternoon, this is a quiet place in the middle of the increasingly noisy Gallatin Valley. And today is a rare day off for me. I have no podcast editing work, no band rehearsals or gigs, and, thankfully, no responsibilities for other people's pets. After several weeks of back-to-back critter sitter gigs, I'm finally free to relax and bask in the soothing sounds of nature, which is why I hesitate before answering a call from Patrick's person. But I'm curious. My next stay with her dog isn't for another month. Why would she need to talk with me now?

"Hey there," I say. "What's going on?"

After the obligatory *How are you? Fine. You?* verbal shuffle, she says, "I'm hoping you can tell me how you got Patrick to behave during his playdate with Grace?" She pauses. "What magic spell did you use on him?"

"Uhm…I didn't do much of anything except drive him out there and open the gate," I reply. "But," I add quickly, "of course I made sure they weren't growling and being aggressive with each other before I let him into the yard with her. I made sure he looked happy, like he wanted to play, not fight."

"Oh," she says. "Hmmm…I wondered how you did that because I want to take him with me to a friend's house and she has a dog."

"Well…" I say, not wanting to give her any advice.

OMG, what have I done! What if she takes Patrick over there and he attacks the other dog, and there's blood, and vet bills?

I take a deep breath before I continue. "All I did, really, that might be out of the ordinary, is talk to him. I told him Grace is a nice dog and that he'd have fun with her. And I told him to be a good boy." I stop talking, stop walking, and look out across the comingling waters. I clench my jaw and wait.

There's a long moment of silence, and then she says, "You figured out the problem with his food and then got him to play with another dog by talking to him. Huh. From now on I'm gonna call you The Dog Whisperer."

CHAPTER FOUR

Discovering Montana

The year 2020, with its pandemic pandemonium, wasn't the first time during the past fifty years that Southwest Montana has been rapidly invaded by enthusiastic immigrants.

In the 1970s, a flock of famous writers and actors found refuge in the Livingston area: Thomas McGuane, Richard Brautigan, Margot Kidder, Jim Harrison, Peter Fonda, Jeff Bridges, Tim Cahill... .

In the 1980s, thousands of members of Church Universal and Triumphant followed Elizabeth Clare Prophet to the Paradise Valley just north of Yellowstone National Park. There they erected prefabricated houses and utilitarian buildings on pristine wildlife habitat near the Gardner River. They also built fallout shelters. They buried fuel storage tanks, which later leaked into the soil and ground water. The shelters were supposed to protect church members from the nuclear war

Elizabeth Clare Prophet had predicted. In March of 1990, members hunkered down in their shelters and waited for an apocalypse that never came. After they resurfaced and Prophet developed Alzheimer's, many of the faithful left the Paradise Valley and melted into the populace of Livingston and Bozeman.

In 1992 and 1994, two popular films starring Brad Pitt and Western Montana's spectacular landscapes—*A River Runs Through It* and *Legends of the Fall*—ignited another real estate boom when hordes of movie fans arrived, looking for a mythic version of The West that has never existed, except in fiction. Before that, in 1991, during the filming of *A River Runs Through It*, cast and crew members augmented their incomes with quick real estate transactions. They bought houses in Montana—cheap by California standards—and re-sold them to friends in L.A. for three times what they'd paid. I heard about this at a party where the people making all the money were bragging to each other. They were so proud of themselves, unaware that, almost overnight, their actions had caused the cost of housing for locals to triple without a commensurate increase in their incomes.

The release of the film *The Horse Whisperer* in 1998 added another layer of mystique to Southwestern Montana. The film was based on a book written by British author Nicholas Evans, who admitted his boyhood addiction to Hollywood westerns. During interviews about his book and the movie version of *The Horse Whisperer*, Evans acknowledged the mystical, metaphoric, and mythic aspects of his stories. But moviegoers took what they saw on the screen literally. They arrived in Montana expecting to encounter stoic cowboys and their adoring horses. Instead, they found small towns populated by conservative-minded folks who depended on agriculture and tourism for their livelihoods. Nary a Starbucks or wine store in sight. Lots of grain elevators and iceberg lettuce, though, as well as bad attitudes toward outsiders.

One day in the late 1990s, a grant writer I knew, and sometimes worked with, announced that he and his wife were moving back to Kentucky, where they were from. "We've been living out here on the frontier for five years now," he said, "and I'm tired of struggling to earn a living."

Wow, I thought: You don't often think of Kentucky as an ample source of financial prosperity, which put Montana's per capita income in grim perspective. That man and his wife left Bozeman. However, most people who moved here stayed— either because they couldn't make enough money to leave or because they had so much money they could leave and return whenever they pleased.

The summer of 2020 eclipsed all previous population surges, however. The pandemic and fans of the Paramount TV series *Yellowstone* fueled a real estate feeding frenzy like nothing Montanans on the west side of the state had ever seen before. Not since the gold rush days of the 1860s, anyway.

After months of sheltering in place, people became restless. The wide-open spaces and clean air in Montana appealed to everyone who wanted to escape crowded cities, masks, and the restrictions of the pandemic. Yellowstone National Park was overrun by enthusiastic, wannabe outdoor recreationists. They trampled vegetation, littered, ignored warnings about thermal pools, and risked their lives trying to take selfies on the edges of cliffs or next to bison, bears, and moose. The national park frenzy was fueled by social media images and blog articles that touted a campervan lifestyle in which glamorous people earned a living from anywhere on the planet. Each post featured an enticing unpopulated landscape in the background. The posts and photos—like the characters and storylines in *Yellowstone*—were pure, highly-improbable fiction. But oh, how deluded viewers yearned to believe.

By the way, until reliable Internet connections were available in Montana, people with enough money to buy land and/ or homes didn't live here full-time, unless they were retired. By the twenty-teens, however, most of Montana had access to high-speed Internet, and most professionals could work remotely—a fact thoroughly proven by the pandemic shut down. That changed everything.

Considering that the pandemic real estate feeding-frenzy didn't begin in earnest until June of 2020, the meteoric rise in the median price of a house in Bozeman during that year was impressive. The cost of a single-family house increased from the mid-$300,000s to nearly $500,000 before the end of 2020. By the end of 2021, a local real estate broker published statistics in *Bozeman Magazine* that showed the median price as $650,000. In October of 2022, a local television reporter stated the average home price in Bozeman as $869,000. Almost overnight, Western Montana became a place where only wealthy people could afford to buy a house. Locals struggled—financially, emotionally, and mentally—with the abrupt changes to their small towns.

One man, Sean Hawksford, became so desperate that he began begging, literally, for someone to sell him a house. He stood on street corners, wearing a sandwich sign made from cardboard. One side read *Please sell me a home* with his email address printed in large black letters. The other side showed a list of checkboxes: *down payment*, check, *financing*, check, *solid income*, check. The final item on the list: *home*. No check mark in that box. He held a third sign in his hand that read, *Local Business Owner, Wife Pregnant, Paid Rent Here For 10 Years, Anything Helps, God Bless*.

By the time Sean took to the streets, he and his wife had made twenty offers on twenty houses. They were pre-approved for a mortgage loan. But whenever they made an offer, someone else swooped in and bought it with cash, usually paying far more than the asking price—sometimes without even seeing the house in person. With a budget max of $500,000, Sean and his wife became desperate. They wanted to get settled into a house before their baby arrived.

During many cold days in October of 2021, Sean stood on sidewalks in downtown Bozeman wearing his sandwich boards and holding his sign. People took pictures and posted them on social media. He gave interviews to newspaper, television, and radio reporters. Bloggers blogged. Talking heads talked. Meanwhile, social media sites teamed with scathing opinions about the "outsiders." Californians were especially vilified online and in person—because they were assumed to be the people with all the cash, although plenty of people from New York, Seattle, Houston, Denver, and elsewhere, bought houses and land in the Bozeman area. Vehicles with California license plates were keyed, and frustrated locals shouted hateful words at the drivers of those vehicles.

Sean became a regional hero, a symbol of the fight against injustice—a member of the ninety-nine percent single-handedly battling the wealthy one percent. He represented the mythical David, a small common man, fighting Goliath. In that story, even though the giant seemed to have all the odds in his favor, David won the fight. Sean also won.

In a follow-up story one year later, KZBK-TV reported, "A homeowner whose family had recently experienced tragedy and loss reached out to the young family, insisting they buy his home." The video showed footage of the Hawksford's house, beginning with the nursery where their baby boy slept—a sweet victory for the common people.

Sean Hawksford's triumph encouraged me, as well. If he could win that colossal battle, which had seemed so daunting at the start, maybe I could, too. That hopeful feeling didn't last long, however. Every day, the cost of everything—groceries, hardware and office supplies, fuel and vehicle maintenance, restaurant meals, etcetera—increased, partly the result of higher wages for workers who had to pay more for housing. A ruthless, vicious circle.

CHAPTER FIVE

California Cats

Maisie died when she was twenty-one years and nine months old. Fortunately (for me), she died a few hours before I was supposed to start taking care of her for a week. If she'd waited until the next day, she would've been the second cat in the same house to die on my watch.

Maisie and her brother, Bosley, lived with my sister, Salli, in Burbank, California. Bosley died in the fall of 2018, during the years I lived with the cats while Salli worked on a television series in Atlanta. She planned to be gone for two months, but then the show got picked up for additional seasons, and two months turned into more than two years. I didn't mind, though. I had portable freelance work, and living in Southern California allowed me to escape Montana winters and explore new places.

In SoCal, I rode my bike year-round, and learned to navigate the Metro so I could check out some of the other eighty-seven cities in Los Angeles County. More than ten million people live in L.A. County—ten times the number of people who live in the entire state of Montana, which is roughly the size of the entire country of Japan. In addition to new places, I could also explore the worlds and ideas inside books.

Because I was a resident of L.A. County, sort of, the Los Angeles Public Library gave me a card, as did the Burbank Library. With those two library cards, I had access to hundreds of thousands of books and audiobooks—in addition to the access I already had with my Missoula and Bozeman library cards. All those libraries have a total of seventy-seven branch locations. For a book nut like me, having four library cards and access to seventy-seven buildings full of books is very exciting.

I found work editing podcasts for several organizations and worked as a temporary assistant for a movie industry executive—a gig that paid a jaw-dropping hourly rate. I joined a Meetup group and learned to play the ukulele. I made new friends who invited me to their social activities. Even though I missed my family and friends in Montana, life in SoCal was good. But then Bosley died.

In his younger days, he'd been a strong and handsome cat, a leggy, long-haired yellow boy with a permanent worried look on his sweet face. Even during his final days, skinny and wobbly, he enjoyed going outside for his morning backyard patrol—at a slow and careful pace. And he was still a lover. At night, Bosley slept on my pillow, next to the back of my head. He usually snuggled close enough for me to feel his heartbeat through my skull.

One morning, I woke at 4 a.m. Something didn't feel right. As I surfaced into conscious awareness, I heard what had awakened me: Bosley struggling to breathe.

It was 7 a.m. in Atlanta, so I texted my sister to tell her I needed to take Bosley to the vet as soon as they opened. By then, she'd been away for more than a year, but I sent her kitty reports and pictures almost every day. She also communicated, often, with the vet who had been caring for her cats since they were kittens. Bosley took medication for hyperthyroidism, and we knew from a past x-ray that he had a tiny mass in his chest. But when I took him in that morning, a new x-ray showed a large mass pressing into his lungs and heart.

After the vet told me this news, she looked at me, waiting. Her manner was compassionate, but she needed me to make a decision. There were three options: 1) surgery, 2) let him struggle to breathe and keep his heart pumping until he could no longer do either, 3) put him down, as the accelerated death of a pet is so inelegantly called. I held Bosley on my lap. I ran my fingers lightly across his boney spine and rubbed his ears, his favorite touchy things. He purred and rubbed his chin against my hand.

"What would you do if this were your cat? I asked her.

She didn't hesitate. "If Bosley were my cat," she said, "I'd let him go."

I felt a sting of tears as I cradled Bosley in my arms. I stood up and slid him gently into his travel crate. "Okay," I said. "I'll call Salli and then let you know what she decides. "Will you come to the house, if letting him go is her decision?" I asked. I couldn't bear the thought of making this sweet cat get into the crate and suffer through another trip to the vet, not to mention the anxiety associated with being in the clinic environment. His last moments.

"Yes," she replied.

■ ■ ■

Friday evening at 9 p.m., shortly after her clinic had closed for the evening, the veterinarian arrived with a small duffle bag. I carried Bosley into my sister's bedroom and laid him on a soft king-sized pillow covered with an old towel. I petted and talked to him while the vet did her work. He died at 9:06 p.m., 12:06 a.m. in Atlanta, the time and place my sister cried.

Bosley's death was heartbreaking for my sister and a low point for me as a pet sitter. I expect some anxiety when I'm responsible for other people's pets. There's always uncertainty. But an animal's death on my watch, even though it's not even remotely my fault, feels awful. As Bosley died, a memory from my past rushed in, blooming bright and painful, creating a terrible ache in the center of my chest.

In 1991, I agreed to care for one cat and four dogs, including an elderly Golden Retriever, while their person took a vacation in Europe. She went to France to ride cross-country on a three-week bicycle tour. In the time before people in Montana, and most of the rest of the world, had cell phones, she was nearly unreachable.

The woman had been gone for two weeks when I found the Golden lying on the concrete floor of the laundry room, no longer able to walk, eat, or drink water. My only option for contacting her was to call the 800 number of the cycling company. I had no Google, no World Wide Web, no cell phone—no way to contact this woman except with wired technology.

Getting a message to her through the travel company took hours. It was afternoon in France when I called and the bikers were out riding, far from towns and phones. Once she received my message, the woman had to contact the vet in Bozeman to give him verbal and faxed permission to treat the dog. And then, the vet had to schedule a time to come to the house. The seven-hour time difference between Montana and France complicated scheduling. The vet arrived at the house twelve hours after I found the poor dog in distress.

I spent most of those hours sitting on the cold concrete floor, holding the dying dog's head in my lap. The experience was beyond horrible. I had no permission to authorize help for this dog. Even if I'd had authorization to take her to the veterinary clinic, I wasn't strong enough, even back then, to pick up a Golden Retriever by myself and put her into a vehicle. The house was eight miles from Bozeman. The nearest neighbor, whom I didn't know, was a long way off. The two friends I tried to call were not at home to answer their phones. In the days of landlines, of course, a person had to be at home to hear the phone ring and answer a call.

I watched the dog suffer and tried to soothe her with soft words as I stroked her fur. I learned from the experience, though, and made sure nothing like this would ever happen again. Each person who's hired me since 1991 has given me authorization to make decisions about their pets in case of an emergency. Of course, now that everyone has a phone in their pocket, it's much easier to deal with a crisis.

When decisions needed to be made for Bosley, my sister was only a text or call away. But I also had written permission, signed by her, to authorize treatment for her cats if she wasn't available. In Burbank, my name and phone number were also on file with the veterinary clinic as a person authorized to make decisions for both cats. People can't always answer their phones, even when it's an emergency.

Experience is sometimes a cruel teacher. It taught me to prepare for the worst by insisting that my clients sign an authorization-for-treatment form. A form doesn't help with distress, however. The animal's or mine.

Most people think caring for other people's pets is an easy way to make money. They are wrong.

CHAPTER SIX

Logistics

Moving into someone else's house for a few days or weeks is like, well, moving. My bag contains all the usual stuff: clothes, shoes and socks, jackets, toiletries, etcetera. But I also need my work equipment, which could include some, or all, of the following: laptop, tablet, Bluetooth speakers, digital recorder, microphones, cables, scripts, headphones, notebooks, pens, draft pages, jump drives, external USB and card reader connectors, work and personal phones, plus charger cables and adaptors for all of the above. The only way I can take most of that equipment with me is by dismantling my home studio/office.

During my job interviews, the people are always delighted when they find out I work part-time and remotely, because they think that means I can be with their pets all day, every day. In their imaginations, I arrive at their house with a laptop and a small bag of clothes. They have no idea.

I also need to bring food. Normally, I buy fresh food several times a week and don't buy more than I need for the next day or two. How the heck am I supposed to know what I'll want to eat next Wednesday? When the apocalypse comes, I'll be the first person to die from starvation. The contents of my refrigerator are barely an excuse to keep electricity flowing through it, and the nonperishable items in the cupboards in my small kitchen don't come close to filling the spaces. I'm an anxiety and project procrastination eater—or rather, overeater—so I don't keep problem foods at home. (Every food that's sweet and creamy or crunchy and salty is a problem food for me.)

Smoothies are my breakfast of choice, which requires a good blender. Most people have a blender, but sometimes they keep it in an odd place, such as the laundry room or in the garage. I try to remember to ask them where it is. My smoothies are complicated concoctions made from fruits, protein powder, and various items from the latest list of superfoods. I eat salads for dinner, which also require fresh ingredients. So, staying in a client's house that's not near a grocery store (and most of them aren't) creates a new set of logistical problems for me. Yes, I am ridiculous about food.

My favorite pillow is also essential, as are supplements, books, musical instruments, and other band equipment for practicing and performing. While I'm away, I don't have my forty-two-inch monitor screen, my studio monitor speakers, or my piano keyboard. I can't compose or arrange music using my digital audio workspace, so creative projects must be delayed or planned for accordingly. For short stays I usually leave my studio/office intact and schedule time to work at home each day—if I'm not staying too far out of town, that is.

My dad used to comment on my inability to exit the house with everything I needed on the first try. He'd laugh and say that I always had to come back into the house at least three times before I'd remembered and collected everything. Even as an experienced house-leaver, this is still a problem for me. Maybe I only go back inside once these days, but I still forget stuff—even though I make a list of everything I'll need during my time away. Since each living situation is unique, and the details of my freelance work projects change often, I must make a new list for each job.

Then I must remember to check that list before I drive away from home.

My tendency to forget to take important stuff with me is an enigma. My memory is excellent. I'm a well-organized, detail-oriented person. I check and double-check the minutiae of work projects. And yet, I often show up at a destination or event without an important item. For example: Last week I arrived at a group sing-along session at the Gallatin Rest Home without my ukulele. I had the empty case with me. Apparently, I'd grabbed the case and trotted confidently out the door, walking right past the ukulele resting on its stand in the living room. When you don't have a regular routine, which I have rarely ever had, it's easy to forget what you need to remember.

I don't like it when people say they're having a "senior moment." Arriving without my ukulele has nothing to do with my age. I forgot stuff when I was a teenager, and I've forgotten stuff at every age since then. But knowing that I've always forgotten stuff doesn't make me feel any better. In fact, it makes me feel worse because it highlights the length of time I've been working on my strategies to overcome this cognitive quirk: decades. Way too long. With minimal success.

Smart phones have helped. I use phone apps for lists, notes, alerts, calendars, and to connect to my files in the cloud, in case I forget to bring whatever device they're stored on to a meeting or appointment. Whenever possible, I use repetitive routines to create habit grooves in my brain. After thirty-five years, I'm really good at remembering to drink a cup of green tea right after I wake up.

Depending on the opinion and experience of the expert, they say it takes anywhere from seven to sixty days to create a new habit. That may be true if you're a person who uses the same routines every day. In that case, you can just stack a new habit on top of an existing habit. But if you're a person whose lifetime record for living in the same house or apartment is three years, and your life circumstances and jobs change often, especially while critter sitting, building consistent habits is beyond challenging.

One of my younger sisters (they're all younger) recently asked me why I've moved and changed jobs so many times. As an adult, she's lived in two houses. I gave her a long list of complicated reasons. Well, they're complicated if you evaluate my decisions on a case-by-case basis, but in their simplest form, they could be compared to the surge of energy that rips through a dog when he spies a deer or a gopher: That looks like fun! Let's go!

Moving from place to place, however—the actual lugging of stuff—is not that much fun. Especially when it's short term and involves living in someone else's house. And yet, I keep doing it. What kind of circle of hell have I created for myself? But, really, what else can I expect from myself? My parents taught me well. Shortly after my thirteenth birthday, my family moved for the sixteenth time. I'm an expert mover.

Recently, I've been doing three or four critter sitter jobs a month. That means I move a bunch of stuff in and out of my condo six to eight times a month. First, of course, I must carry the everything out of my condo and put it into my vehicle. Second, of course, I must carry all that same stuff from the vehicle into someone else's house. Third and fourth, I must do all that in reverse. This takes a lot of time, but I try not to think of it as wasted time. Instead, I focus on the exercise that's built into my lifestyle. Each day involves a lot of picking up and carrying, which keeps my arms, glutes, and heart in pretty good condition. If not for those darn crunchy knees, I'd be in excellent shape.

Other people might exercise their brains with crosswords and sudoku puzzles. My brain exercises itself by working out what I should take with me every time I leave a place—mine or someone else's. Each day involves a lot of remembering: where specific items are, what ought to go with me, and how to organize my time efficiently. Some days, I'm a rock star remember-er, and some days I arrive with an empty ukulele case.

Every day, I wonder how my life might be different, what I might accomplish, if only I would/could stay in one place and stop moving in and out of other people's houses every few days.

CHAPTER SEVEN

Zak, Tia, and Rocky: A Russian White and His German Shepherds

I hear the dogs long before I see them. They bark and growl as I steer my small SUV onto the edge of the asphalt driveway. They bark and growl as I sit, staring through the windshield, ogling the spectacular view of the Gallatin Valley and surrounding mountain ranges. They bark and growl as I walk toward the large Tuscan-style house perched on the west flank of the Bridger Mountains.

The curved walkway is lined with well-tended flowering bushes and native grasses. Near the front door, a wooden rocking chair covered by a flowered cushion stands next to a small metal table. It looks like an inviting place for morning coffee and contemplation. Or it could be, without the barking dogs.

Through expansive, floor-to-ceiling windows, I see a matching pair of German Shepherds leaping and snarling with a vigorous determination to defend their house from my intrusion. Propped against a section of window glass is a sign that declares, *Beware: German Shepherd on Duty*, which seems quite unnecessary. The closer I get to the house, the more frantically furious the dogs become. Nothing about them looks one bit friendly. For a moment, I consider leaving, despite my invitation to be here for an interview.

A trim, middle-aged woman with short salt and pepper hair opens the door when I'm still ten feet away. Of course she does. No need to ring a bell or knock on a door at this house. The dogs bolt past her and rush outside, circling my legs. The volume and intensity of their growling and barking increases, although I wouldn't have thought that was possible.

"Come in!" the woman shouts over the canine din, waving me forward.

She acts like everything's normal. For her, I guess it is. I follow her into a spacious entryway, adopting a sideways gait to keep an eye on the snarling dogs. The skin on my legs feels taut, like it's on high alert, expecting teeth to break through it and go for the bones underneath at any second.

I pull a deep breath into my lungs and solar plexus. As we walk, I focus on the woman's sporty sandals and her thick hair. I think about where she might have bought those sandals and refresh my lifelong, futile desire for thicker hair. Inside the house, I take another deep breath and contemplate a large, noisy abstract painting on one of the walls. The woman pushes the massive, ornate wooden door shut and turns to me.

"This is Tia," she says, pointing to the German Shepherd with the orange collar.

"Hey, Tia," I say, leaning slightly toward her, extending a damp palm out a couple of inches—my non-dominant hand, just in case. Tia doesn't seem at all pleased to meet me. She backs away, woofing.

The woman swings her arm toward the other dog. "And this is Rocky. You can always tell its him because his collar is black."

Rocky is even less pleased to meet me. He bares his teeth and snarls, leaning back until most of his weight is on his hind legs. He looks like he's ready to launch at my throat. Instinctively, I angle away from him.

"Be nice!" the woman says, calmly.

Calmly! While I'm about to be mauled, she is calm. Rocky ignores her command and continues expressing his displeasure with a series of threatening growls while we walk into an enormous kitchen/dining room with ridiculously high ceilings.

German Shepherds are inherently loyal and loving dogs. I know this. The first dog I ever lived with as an adult was a German Shepherd. Jeena was sweet, loving, and smart enough to learn how to ride with me on my small motorcycle—a Honda CB175. She sat between my legs as I drove, gripping the gas tank with her claws to stay upright around corners. We were a spectacle cruising the streets of Miles City, Montana, in 1972.

Despite my history with and love for German Shepherds, I'm a little freaked out by these two dogs. Amid the mayhem of aggression and barking, an ancient instinct urges me to flee. I keep reminding myself that German Shepherds are lovers. Jeena behaved exactly like Rocky: fierce when anyone tried to enter my apartment, but docile and sweet-natured when she felt safe. My experience, up until this moment, anyway, matches what I know about the history of the breed.

In her book, *Rin Tin Tin*, Susan Orlean chronicled the development of German Shepherd dogs by Max Emil Friedrich von Stephanitz in 1899. She writes, "This new breed, von Stephanitz imagined, would be… smart, athletic, and loyal to the bone."

It all began with a dog named Hektor whom von Stephanitz described as "the maddest rascal the wildest ruffian and incorrigible provoker of strife; never idle, always on the go; well disposed to harmless people, but no cringer, mad about children and always in love." Nearly one hundred and twenty-five years later, Rocky is an excellent example of von Stephanitz's success at breeding for loyalty and loving devotion.

There's no doubt in my mind about Rocky's loyalty to, and love for, his person. I'm sure he will fight to the death for this woman. His athletic moves also display an abundance of the "wildest ruffian" and "provoker of strife" traits of Hecktor, his first ancestor. My heart races while I remind myself to present myself as one of the "harmless people" he is genetically inclined to love. He's just doing his job, I tell myself, along with a reminder to *breathe*.

In the kitchen/dining room, I gawk at immense white marble countertops and tastefully ornate cream-colored cabinets, while trying to focus on what the woman is telling me about her expectations for a pet sitter. Meanwhile, Tia and Rocky carry on with their vocal protests. Mid-sentence, she suddenly turns to the dogs and says, firmly, "Rocky. Tia. Stop it."

They do not stop.

To me she says, "Please sit," and points to a dining table—a massive, highly polished wooden plank that could easily accommodate twelve. I sit. At least one of us is obeying commands.

The moment my butt hits the chair, Tia goes quiet and slinks over to sniff at my legs and feet. "They are really nice dogs," the woman says, "once they get to know you." She sits on the chair at the head of the table and inspects me with mild curiosity.

"I'm sure they are," I say weakly. "We'll get along fine." This is my moment to demonstrate confidence. So, I extend my left hand toward Tia, palm up, fingers flat. "Hey, girl," You're okay." She sniffs each of my fingers thoroughly. Slowly, I move my hand to her neck and drag my fingernails lightly underneath her stiff orange collar. She sighs and leans in. Whew! One dog down.

Rocky suddenly stops barking, but his growls are now deeper and more menacing. His stance is tight and tilted forward. I keep my eyes on him as I move my hands higher on Tia's head and rub her ears. She moans softly. Rocky stops growling and begins to creep toward me. But then the woman stands, and he backs away.

"I'll show you around," she says, walking toward a tall pair of glass doors that open onto a flagstone patio.

I get up and start walking after her. The dogs rush to the door and wait eagerly for her to open it. As I pass the wide, arched doorway into the living room, I see a scratching post tower—a vertical mansion of carpeted shelves and enclaves at least seven feet high. It looks completely out of place next to a high-end leather sofa and custom-made coffee table. Lying on the top platform is a white, short-haired cat. I stop walking.

"What an unusual-looking cat," I say.

"That's Zak," says the woman, pausing to look at him. At the sound of her voice saying his name, Zak opens one golden eye, stares at me for two seconds, and then returns to his nap. All the white cats I've ever seen have had long hair: Persians, Angoras, Himalayans, Siberians. Later, I find out that Zak is a Russian White, a cat bred to have a beautiful, snow-white coat. Breeding success achieved!

The dogs follow us around the yard for about a minute, and then Rocky loses interest in me. He sniffs bushes and stiff brown tufts of grass as we walk toward a patio area. There, a custom-built, wood-fired, brick pizza oven squats next to a small Aspen grove. There's an oversized four-car garage attached to this side of the house. We go inside so the woman can show me the stash of extra pet supplies. Also in there: two vintage cars, four mountain bikes, several pairs of skis, and a plethora of hiking and fishing gear.

Another garage sits about fifty feet from the house, near the beginning of the long driveway. An outdoor stairway leads up to a wide wooden deck and a green door.

"That's the guest house," the woman says, pointing across the yard. "Right now, one of my husband's colleagues is staying there."

"Oh?" I say, pondering this new information. We're eight miles out of town, and the nearest neighbor is about a mile down the dirt road.

The woman glances at my face, and then explains: "He's waiting to get into a house he bought. The closing is next week, the day after you arrive."

"Ah, that's good to know," I say, relieved. And then I realize she must have decided to hire me, since she's just informed me that I'll "arrive" the day before the tenant leaves.

Even though I'm still a bit apprehensive about Rocky's behavior, this is good news. My fees increase with additional pets, so taking care of three animals will give me a nice payday. Once the dogs transfer their loyalty to me, being out here alone won't be a concern. I'm starting to understand why the woman chose German Shepherds as pets. *Two* German Shepherds. Even an expert burglar with a gun would have trouble shooting both dogs before one of them ripped into his throat.

As it turns out, I never needed to worry about the man staying in the guest house. He's nice. And helpful.

■ ■ ■

I have an appointment with Guest House Man at 7 a.m. When I steer my small SUV onto the long driveway, I pass a green drift boat on a trailer that's hitched to a tan Toyota pickup truck. There's fly fishing gear in the cab.

Apparently, Rocky loves Guest House Man, which is why he's been recruited to help me get into the house without experiencing a violent death by German Shepherd teeth. The owners had to leave for the airport at 4 a.m.—too early, they thought, for me to show up—although I would have done it because I start getting paid the moment I arrive at a client's house. The presence of this man, even though he's a total stranger, eases my anxiety as Rocky goes through his barky, growly, snarly routine when I enter the house. Tia only barks for a few seconds and then accepts some ear scratching from me while we wait for Rocky to calm down.

"Shut up, Rocky!" Guest House Man finally yells. "God, I would *never* have a German Shepherd as a pet," he says.

Wow. I can't think of a graceful verbal response to that declaration. I wonder if this man's hosts know about his hostility toward their beloved pets.

He walks to the marble countertop covering the expansive kitchen island and picks up a large, clear plastic container half full of dried catnip treats. He points at it. "If you can't find Zak," he says, "just shake these treats and he'll come running. That cat is her pride and joy," he says, in a tone that seems like a warning.

Oh, great. How will I keep track of a young cat that roams twenty-two hilly acres filled with tall grasses, bushes, and trees? A new layer of anxiety settles onto my existing anxiety about keeping other people's pets safe while they're away.

Meanwhile, Zak looks down on us from his scratching post mansion. Through the arched doorway that opens into the living room, I can see him lying, majestic and aloof, on the highest carpeted platform, eyes half open, a bored but curious expression on his exotic face.

Guest House Man opens a door in the pantry cabinet and points to a bag of dog treats inside. "There are more in the laundry room," he says.

"Good to know," I say, grabbing the bag. Rocky stops growling and points his nose upward, sniffing while he circles my legs.

The man points an index finger down at the dogs. "Stay," he says. He turns his back on us and walks down the hallway toward the door that opens into the garage.

Evidently, we are done.

"Thanks," I call after him. He raises an arm and keeps walking. Rocky starts to follow but stops when the door closes behind the man.

Tia decides I'm not a threat after we're alone for ten seconds. She leans against my left leg. Rocky continues to circle me, and now her, emitting low growls. But when the stiff plastic crackles as I open the bag of dog treats, he suddenly goes quiet. I carry the bag to the dining room and sit on the same chair I sat on during my interview. Tia and Rocky follow me, their noses pointed at the bag.

"Sit," I say in my most authoritative voice. They both sit, immediately. "Stay," I command. They stay. After taking a deep, fear-controlling breath, I reach into the bag, pull out two treats, and extend them, one in each hand, toward the dogs. They accept the treats politely. My fingers remain attached to my hands. I relax a little and reach into the bag for more. Yay for dog treats! Five treats later, Rocky turns into Velcro Dog.

■ ■ ■

Zak emerges from a row of bushes with something clamped between his teeth—something struggling. It takes a moment for me to identify it as a baby rabbit. Zak ambles toward the patio on the kitchen side of the house (not the one with the pizza oven) where Rocky and I are sitting together on an outdoor wicker couch. The cat is utterly unconcerned by the fuzzy little legs kicking the air underneath his chin. He stops near the kitchen door, which, thankfully, I had the presence of mind to close when we all came out to the patio an hour ago. Zak waits for the door to open, for an opportunity to present his gift.

"Sorry, not gonna happen," I say.

I quickly free myself from Rocky's hairy embrace and stand up. If the bunny isn't mortally wounded, I want to save it. But I'm too slow.

Tia jumps up from her lookout post—the place at the top of the hill where she can monitor what's happening in the field and on the dirt road leading to the house, a place from which she can be on continuous alert to verbally berate any hawk or hot air balloon bold enough to invade *her* airspace. She trots over to Zak and sniffs at the bunny. Zak drops it (gift delivered), and the bunny tries to hop away. But Tia quickly grabs it in her own teeth and runs down the hill that slopes west, away from the flagstone patio. Zak sprints after her. In a sloping field of native grasses, cut short by a power mower, Zak and Tia begin a gruesome game of keep away.

I ponder my options, none of which seem viable. There's no way I can chase after and catch a dog or a cat that doesn't want to give up a prize. A lifetime of chasing after critters in houses, yards, parks, and on trails has taught me that lesson.

"Tia! Zak!" I yell. They ignore me. Running after them in a lumpy, hilly field would be futile, especially in this heat. The weather app on my phone predicts a high temperature of ninety-nine degrees by four o'clock this afternoon. I look away from the doomed bunny and focus on the view.

This is a beautiful place to hang out. From the patio, I can see three of the four mountain ranges that surround the Gallatin Valley: Spanish Peaks to the west, Gallatin Range to the south, and the Big Belt Mountains to the north. The fourth range, the Bridgers, rises directly behind me. Sunsets must be magnificent from this house, which sits high in the foothills under the tower of Baldy Mountain. Both the driveway and the floor-to-ceiling windows offer spectacular views of the entire valley.

After Guest House Man left us this morning, I found a pair of binoculars on a side table in the living room. Through the lenses, I could see all the way to the confluence of the Missouri River near the town of Three Forks, more than thirty miles from Bozeman. Or did I only imagine that place as I scanned a line of dark green treetops? I'm not sure, but everything I see is a magnificent statement about why so many people want to live here. Improvements to Internet technology and more direct flights to more major cities offer conveniences new residents need—services that allow them to enjoy a glorious immersion into natural beauty while maintaining their big-city connections to people, work, and life-styles.

It used to be time-consuming and frustrating to get in and out of the Gallatin Valley, and the Internet was unreliable—mostly dial-up in rural areas until around the year 2010. That's why it remained a small town for so long. Until recently, there were very few direct flights from the Bozeman airport to anywhere except Denver, Seattle, Minneapolis, and Salt Lake City. But the demand for flights has grown, markedly, during the past ten years. Now, we can fly direct to Burbank, Los Angeles, and San Francisco, California; Dallas and Houston, Texas; Portland, Oregon; Las Vegas, Chicago, Phoenix, Philadelphia, Nashville, Atlanta, Boston, New York, and New Jersey. Every flight added makes it easier for people to come and go, and to live here part-time. I fear the consequences. Houses, condos, and commercial buildings are rising from fields at an alarmingly rapid rate. The big money that developers offer to farmers in the valley these days has made it more attractive for them, or their heirs, to sell the land.

I gaze out at our beautiful valley—referred to as the *Valley of Flowers* by indigenous people—while Zak and Tia end the hapless bunny's life in the field below. When I turn back to the couch, I see Rocky staring at me, head tilted, a quizzical expression on his face. He's not interested in the bunny, or anything else in the yard right now. He is only interested in being exactly where I am. He wants me to get back on the couch or to let him know what's next. I walk over and sit, giving his ears a rub as I pick up the book I was reading before the bunny horror show began. Rocky lays his big head on my thigh.

The couch is shaded by a small grove of trees, protecting us from the mid-morning sun. I close my eyes and breathe in the scent of green leaves and dried grasses. And, of course, *olor o perro.* I shift slightly to reposition an aching knee. Rocky heaves a huge sigh and scrunches his body closer to my hip.

Looking at him now, it's difficult to remember he's the same dog that threatened to tear me into tiny, bloody bits less than three hours ago, and last week. Perhaps he's added me to his "loyal to" list. I hope so. But I won't know for sure until I leave the house for a few hours and then try to come back in again.

Every critter sitter job comes with unpredictable behaviors and personalities—from pets *and* humans. None, that I can recall anyway, has been quite as unsettling as Rocky's behavior. But it's up to me to calm fearful pets and outsmart the tricksters since I'm not hired to change their behavior. I'm just here to make sure they're well cared for and help them feel as safe as possible while their people are away. Rocky seems to have received the message that he's safe with me. Fingers crossed.

I read to the end of the chapter and then gently lift Rocky's head from my damp thigh. Whew, it's hot. I stand up and stretch before walking away from the shade. The stainless-steel bowl sitting under an outdoor faucet needs refilling. Tia and Zak abandon the limp baby rabbit and come running when they hear the water begin to sputter and gush.

■ ■ ■

There's a creek running through this property. The water flows from high up in the Bridger Mountains, sourced from snowpack run-off and underground springs. During my interview tour, the woman pointed out a wide grass path leading from the dirt road to the creek below. It looks like whoever does the mowing around here maintains an access path so animals and people can get to both sides of the creek from the road.

After a dinner of green salad and lavender ice cream, I decide to go exploring. The sun is descending toward the mountains, and the air has begun to cool. It's probably only eighty-five degrees now, instead of a hundred.

"Anybody wanna go for a walk?" I ask the pets sprawled across the kitchen floor's cool terracotta tiles. Rocky and Tia jump up immediately. The door to the patio is open, so they run outside and wait for me to pull on my shoes. Zak stands, stretches, and saunters out through the doorway. I assume he'll see us off and then return to his nap. But no.

As we walk down the driveway, I glance back several times to see Zak trotting along behind us. He's still with us when we reach the dirt road. I remember the story Dana told me about why these people needed a critter sitter to stay in their house.

They used to take the dogs to a boarding kennel. And then the woman decided to get a cat. Maybe they had a mouse problem? Probably so. Normally, owls, snakes, coyotes, and hawks would keep the rodent population in check. But often, after their habitat has been disturbed by bulldozers, construction crews, guard dogs, and property owners, those predators find somewhere else to live. After Zak arrived, he and the German Shepherds quickly became best pals. The first time Rocky and Tia went to the kennel, and the people left Zak home alone, he became deeply depressed, which upset the woman. So now, here I am.

Zak keeps to one side of the road, trotting through the shady patches of grasses and shrubs. Rocky and Tia sniff everything on the uphill side of the road. They run up and down, thoroughly investigating plants, rocks, and soil. It's still very hot, and they are running in fur. Oof.

I turn around to check on Zak. The thought of anything happening to the woman's "pride and joy" terrifies me, but it's kind of hilarious that he's hiking with us. "Hey, Zak. How you doin'?" I stop walking to let him catch up to me. When he's next to my legs, I reach down to scratch his back. "Wanna ride?" I ask. I pick him up and walk on. He accepts a short ride but then squirms to get down. He has instinctive cat stuff to do. I keep an eye on him while he weaves in and out of the tall grasses next to the road.

Rocky and Tia know exactly where we're going. By the time Zak and I reach the mown path that leads down the hill and into the bushes growing next to the creek, the dogs are frolicking in the water. Someone has placed large stones and logs across the creek to create a shallow pond. Rocky and Tia splash through the pond and then flop onto their bellies, lapping water and working their noses to gather information about who's been here recently.

The air inside this grove of trees is cool and moist, a refreshing relief after a hot, dry-as-a-bone day. Zak and I sit together on one of three sky-blue, plastic Adirondack chairs lined up along the bank of the creek. He stretches out next to my leg, purring and lightly panting. His tiny pink tongue looks so innocent. I try not to think about its participation in the recent murder of the baby bunny.

65

I close my eyes and lean my head back against the chair. The sound of running water and whirring insects is soothing. A whisper of breeze ruffles leaves on the Aspen trees. I can hear the dogs splashing and snuffling. We all linger in this cool paradise until the sun begins to touch the Spanish Peaks.

During our walk back toward the house, I'm so mesmerized by the sunset's stunning colors that I forget to pay attention to where Zak is. But he's paying attention to where I am. The quiet evening air is suddenly pierced by a mournful yowl. Oh, my gosh, Zak! I turn around and see him far behind us, trotting along the side of the road, yowling, and hurrying to catch up. He seems upset.

"Sorry!" I shout and start walking back toward him. He quits yowling.

The way back to the house is uphill. There are lots of hills on this high rumple of land. This time Zak lets me carry him all the way to the beginning of the asphalt driveway. I hold him securely but slightly away from my body. He feels very hot.

The cat is nowhere near as hot as the second floor of the house, however.

■ ■ ■

All the bedrooms in this house are upstairs. It's at least twenty degrees hotter there than downstairs. None of the animals will come up when I tell them it's time for bed. They know better. After a quick cold shower, I open the window above my assigned bed—a single-width daybed at one end of a huge room filled with home gym equipment. I'm hoping the wind now whipping ferociously across the side of the mountain will cool the place. I also roll open the window in the bathroom located at the other end of the gym. Cross ventilation. Perfect.

Not perfect. I thrash around on the short, narrow mattress. Falling asleep is not one of my best skills, even in my own comfy bed. My tall body needs more space. This small bed with an uncomfortable mattress is nowhere near my happy place, to say the least. Ten minutes in, I already know that getting to sleep is going to be an issue. I have Ambien and Tylenol PM in my bag, but I try not to take them. I wait to swallow any of those tablets until I've exhausted (intentional pun) all other choices. Nothing important is on tomorrow's schedule, so I decide not to use drugs.

I get off the bed and slide a folded blanket underneath the sheet as a mattress cushion. Better. I rearrange the two, flat pillows (I wish I'd remembered to bring my own) and eventually get comfortable. Mostly. Even though the wind slamming against the house is noisy, the cool air feels wonderful. But then, a sudden gust of wind blows the screen out of the window frame. It falls onto my face. Ouch!

As I'm kneeling on the bed, trying to push the screen back into place, I hear the screen blow out of the bathroom window. It clatters onto the tile floor. The screen above the bed won't stay fastened to the window's frame track, but I shove it into place and roll the window nearly shut, just to find out if a sliver of cool air is a possibility. I wait for the next gust. The screen stays put, but the noise from the wind blasting through the small vertical crack is jarring. Not something I'll ever be able to sleep through.

In the bathroom, I can see that this screen will never stay put. The flimsy metal frame is warped, and the latches are broken. This house is large and Italian-villa-stylish, but it is not new. Replacing windows on the second floor should definitely be added to the owners' home maintenance list. What good is having oodles of money if you can't open the windows in your house? Fresh air must have been one of their priorities when these people chose to live on the side of a mountain, far from a town and neighbors. Or maybe they were only after privacy. I leave the screen on the floor while I contemplate my options.

Wait. This is a huge house. Why should I have to sleep on a daybed in the home gym?

I walk down the wide hallway at the top of the stairs and start opening doors. There's an office/bedroom, a guest bedroom, and a master suite. Inside those rooms are three queen- and king-sized beds. In the master bedroom, I see a portable AC machine connected to a makeshift vent in a small window. Should I go sleep in there? I stand in the doorway, thinking. No, the woman told me to sleep in the gym. She must have a reason. Right? On the day of my interview, she didn't include this side of the second floor in my tour of the house. She simply pointed to the daybed, showed me the bathroom next to the home gym, and said I could sleep there and use that bathroom.

Back in the gym, I consider leaving the screens off the windows to let the cool air blow in, but quickly discard the idea.

Open windows would let bats, leaves, insects, early morning birds, and other flying things inside the house. Nope. I roll both windows shut. There *must* be a fan around here somewhere.

After a short search, I find a small fan sitting on a window ledge in the library area at the top of the stairs. I move equipment away from the walls near the daybed until I find an outlet. I plug in the fan and switch it on. The blades start turning and throw hot air over me. Moving hot air is better than stagnant hot air, I guess. Maybe.

By the time I'm back on the bed and settled in again, it's nearly midnight. Shit. The dogs will be up at dawn. It's definitely too late now to take a sleeping pill. I lie on the bed and listen to the wind pummel the house. I feel sticky and sweaty. There's no way I can fall asleep in this heat. And then, because I'm an incorrigible optimist, I reach up and roll the window open again—just a teeny tiny bit. Immediately, the screen hits my forehead on its way to the floor. Wind slams in through the opening so hard I'm afraid it will tear the window off its hinges. I quickly roll it shut. But, oh, the air that came in for a second felt so refreshing and cool!

What if I go outside to sleep on the patio couch? Another bad idea. The dogs would bark their heads off if I left them inside alone, and Zak would freak if we went outside without him. If they all went out with me, the dogs would bark, and Zak would go off hunting and might get carried off by an owl. Bears and coyotes live around here.

I sigh, wipe sweat off my face with a pillowcase, and breathe through a familiar pattern: breathe in, two, three, four, hold for seven counts, breathe out for eight counts. I make a mental gratitude list: sunshine, well-behaved German Shepherds, clean water on demand, avocados, critter sitter income... .

An hour later, I grab my phone and poke around on YouTube until I find the sleep story about the lavender fields in Provence, France. I listen to it through the Bluetooth speaker connected to my phone. The lavender story is comforting. The male narrator's voice is deep and sonorous. "You'll smell it before you even see it, that unmistakable aroma that fills your nose. It seeps into your senses, instantly mellowing into a smooth and soothing scent. You breathe deeply, inhaling and exhaling this floral cloud...you feel your body begin to release its pent-up tension..."

For the first time ever, I hear the end of the lavender story. It's after 3 a.m. when I finally fall asleep.

Zak wakes me before dawn, when I feel him purring against my leg and kneading my hip with his paws. I open one eye. A pale gray light seeps through the glass of the east-facing window above me. It's way too early. Ugh. I turn my head to look out into the forest of gym equipment. Tia and Rocky are lying a few feet from the bed, heads up, staring at me. When they see me move, they jump up and run over to lick my face. They present the best of German Shepherd traits: friendly, "always on the go; well disposed to harmless people...always in love."

There's no growling or barking. I am their favorite person. It feels good to begin a sleep-deprived day with this small victory.

CHAPTER EIGHT

Navigating Instability

Two of my friends, Shan and Ann, grew up together in Michigan. They have known each other since second grade—a fact I can barely comprehend. I went to eight different schools between kindergarten and high school: Vernonia and Medford in Oregon; Seattle, Wapato, and Yakima in Washington State; Concord, California; New Town, North Dakota; and Miles City, Montana. Along with math, reading, writing, and social studies, I learned the art of navigating instability.

Not included in my education—or modeled for me by the adults who managed my childhood—were social skills or the skills required for attracting and maintaining friendships. Strategies and adults to help me deal with my emotions were also missing. So, I invented my own ways to handle my feelings. Not successfully, of course, since I was a child with no skills or perspective.

Whenever we moved away from classmates or kids in our neighborhood that I had just begun to care about, I pretended they were dead—the best childish idea I could come up with to deal with emotional pain. I didn't know much about death, except that dead people disappeared. In the days before cell phones and the Web, I never saw my classmates or friends again, so imagining them dead made perfect sense to me. In fact, the strategy of pretending people were dead worked for me all the way through high school, and beyond.

Until my mid-thirties, the only direct experience I had with death happened when I was six years old, when Great Grandpa Newman died. Several years before, my family had lived with him for a short time in his small house in Molalla, Oregon. He carried butterscotch candies in his pocket. What I remember is unwrapping and eating the candy, not an emotional attachment to the man.

Great Grandpa Newman died when we lived in Seattle, while my dad earned a Master of Social Work degree at the University of Washington. As a six-year-old, my concept of death was... well, limited to Bible stories. The words "funeral" and "dead" had no linguistic relationship to my direct life experience. And so, with no suspicion of what was about to happen, I jumped for joy when my daddy said I could go with him to the funeral. We would be together for two whole days and one whole night without my four sisters and mother. Just my daddy and me. Bliss!

During the car trip from Seattle to Molalla, I sat on the front seat, perched on top of my square overnight suitcase, watching the scenery glide by, saturated with pleasure.

At the funeral, however, my pleasure drained away as I wandered through a forest of adult legs and endured sticky kisses. The grim minister droned on and on. The shiny wood casket with the stiff, unanimated man lying inside terrified me. That man did not look like the grandpa who had held me on his lap and helped me unwrap pieces of yellow candy. I couldn't connect what I saw to anything I understood. And so, I made up a better story.

When I got home, I told my sisters that Great Grandpa Newman jumped out of the casket during the funeral service and ran away. I told them that all the people in the church chased him down the street to catch him and put him back into the casket. Did I do any damage to the minds of my four little sisters with that story? Probably not. They were all under five years old, and like pre-funeral me did not understand the words *death, funeral,* or *casket.* They certainly didn't know why Great Grandpa Newman's death mattered. It didn't matter to us. We only cared about finding ways to get our parents' attention and guarding whatever bit of domestic space we'd managed to claim for ourselves.

Throughout my childhood, we lived in small two- and three-bedroom houses. I was sixteen years old when we finally moved into a house large enough for me to have my own bedroom—the first time I'd ever experienced private space. As an adult, the largest house I've ever owned or rented measured about twenty-two hundred square feet. When I consider that information, it's easier to understand why I've often felt uncomfortable in other people's huge houses during the past few months: I'm not used to all that space.

It's not that I don't appreciate the architecture and interior design of those large houses. They are all beautiful. It's just that they don't feel cozy. Their high ceilings, huge rooms, and vast expanses of glass and metal feel cavernous, the opposite of cozy. And during late fall, winter, and early spring these houses are cold. That much open space is difficult to keep warm, no matter what heating system is used—except for radiant in-floor heating, which hasn't been available in any of the houses I've stayed in. So far, anyway. I love the floor heat in my condo. The last time I looked for a place to live, in-floor heating topped my list. I like warm and cozy.

What's even less attractive to me is that none of these huge houses include an inviting place to read or write. I need a comfy chair and a lamp. At the very least, a bedside lamp available for nighttime reading. But there are none. I guess cozy and comfortable has gone out of fashion because the newly built houses I've been in feature large, open spaces. It's like the occupants expect to entertain crowds of people, frequently and lavishly. Dana told me she feels the same way about most of the houses she's stayed in. She rarely finds a lamp positioned next to a comfortable chair. I get it: people who read on screens don't need lamps and people who don't read at all don't need lamps. But I like books and reading lamps.

Another thing that bothers me is that there are never more than three people living in these houses. Most of them are occupied by only two people. A six- or ten-thousand-square-foot house inhabited by two or three people just feels wrong to me. Maybe "wrong" is the wrong word, but I feel cold (literally) and somewhat insecure in a sprawling house with twenty-five-foot-high ceilings. Perhaps my uneasiness is related to childhood when my family of nine was crammed into very small houses.

A few years ago, I drove through the Yakima Valley to find the house my family lived in during 1963, my fifth-grade year. In that house, located seven miles from Toppenish, Washington, my four sisters and I shared one bedroom. Three of us slept in a triple bunkbed. The other two slept in single beds. The bottom bed of the triple bunk, where I slept, slid out from under the frame at bedtime, essentially covering all the remaining floor space. So, if one of my sisters decided to get out of bed after we were all in for the night, they stepped on my bed—on me—to get out of the room.

I can't imagine where we put all our clothes and personal items, not that we had many. My parents and my two little brothers slept in a room that wasn't actually a bedroom. It was a walled-in back porch. We used the other, real, bedroom as a music room. In there, a huge, ornately carved, wooden upright piano filled one wall—Great Grandpa Newman's piano.

Music was important to our parents. They sang to each other at their wedding. Our mother taught us to sing three-part harmony before we were even in grade school. Two of my sisters and I sang in church, and people who *never* applauded in God's Hallowed House of Worship applauded for us—three small girls with golden voices, perfect pitch, and a blend of heavenly harmonies. We took piano lessons and practiced in the music room every day after school—otherwise we didn't get our weekly allowance. So, yes, even if five children had to share one bedroom, we had a music room.

Until the day I located that former house near Toppenish, the living/dining room loomed large in my memory. It contained a second piano, an electric organ, a black and white television, and enough floor space for us to sit on chairs or sprawl across the carpet while we watched *Lawrence Welk* and *Gunsmoke* on Saturday evenings after dinner. But when I found the house, I saw that it was unbelievably tiny.

I arrived on a Sunday, when no one else was around. Behind the house, where an old barn and several outbuildings used to be, five shiny construction vehicles were parked in a tidy row. The grass in the yard had been replaced with gravel. The buildings looked freshly painted, gleaming white in the midday sunshine. I parked my car and walked around, peering through windows into the little rooms. No wonder the words my mother spoke most often were, "Go outside and play." I tried to imagine seven energetic children, all under the age of ten, careening around the place. My poor mother.

The living/dining room had been converted into office space. That room, which I remembered as so large, was entirely filled by two normal-sized desks, a row of filing cabinets, and two side chairs. The rooms where we had slept now stored a few pieces of office equipment and boxes of supplies. Neither looked large enough to accommodate a queen-sized bed and one single dresser.

During the past twenty years, I've searched for a few of the houses we lived in when I was a kid. I really wish I hadn't found any of them, though, because, after seeing them, it's more difficult for me to conjure a clear picture of what I experienced in those places. My old memories are muddied by what I saw as an adult. And I don't have any childhood friends to help me remember.

CHAPTER NINE

Zak, Tia, and Rocky: No One Is Thinking of You. Ever.

My second stay with Zak, Tia, and Rocky happens during the blazing heat of late July. I bring a bed sheet from home and spread it over the duvet on the king-sized bed in the master suite. No more daybed in the one-hundred-degree gym room for me, I don't care what my instructions were. Now I can sleep in the comfort of a cool room. They will never know—hee hee hee. About thirty minutes before I'm ready to go to bed, I turn on the portable AC unit. The critters and I sleep well that night.

The next morning, Zak the Killer Cat arrives on the patio with another prize: a small garter snake. This time, I haven't remembered to shut the kitchen door. I abruptly disturb Rocky's snuggle time by jumping off the patio sofa, yelling "No!" I hurry toward the open doorway. I do not want to try to find a snake that's slithering around in this huge house. But after Zak responds to my loud voice by dropping the snake, I can see that its headless and quite dead. Eeeew, did he eat the head? This must be documented. I pull out my phone.

It's my practice to take lots of pictures of the pets. I love photography, and my Samsung phone takes gorgeous photos. At least once a day, I send pics to the people who hired me, along with a brief pet update. People like these messages. They prove I'm on the job, and that their pets are safe and happy while they're away.

The first day I arrive at a house, I always make the animals pose for an "I'm here" shot. On the last day of my stay, I send the people a picture with a message about how eager their pets are to see them. Sometimes I make up a story about what a pet is thinking, based on the expression on its face. I am the storyteller, and the pets are my characters. These moments of creativity are my favorite part of the job.

I send a text to the woman and attach a photo of Zak and his snake. I also tell her about last week's bunny tragedy.

She responds immediately: *As you found out, Zak will bring in animals. He is not allowed to torture or eat them. If they are alive, I transplant them to where they can get away and make all the animals come inside for a few minutes. If they are dead, I throw it down over the embankment to the south of the patio.*

Oh, goodie. A delightful animal carcass disposal duty I wasn't aware of when I took this job.

I go into the kitchen to search for a pair of rubber gloves, which I find in the cabinet under the kitchen sink. Using

79

latex-clad fingers, I carefully pick the snake up by its tail and start toward the south side of the yard, which drops sharply downhill and into a ravine. Rocky, Tia, and Zak follow me, ready for a game of Fetch The Snake. Oops.

"Come on," I say, "into the house with you." The two German Shepherds and their cat immediately go inside. They really are lovely and well-trained critters—well, except for the hostile greetings when I enter the house, a protective response that the woman has probably encouraged. I close the kitchen door on their eager faces and go back to the edge of the hill to fling the unfortunate snake into the air above the grassy slope.

"Time for a walk," I say when I open the kitchen door again. Rocky and Tia follow me out to the driveway, ready for a swim in the cool creek water. But Zak decides it's much too hot for a walk under the blazing sun on a dusty road. Smart cat. He slides into a thick stand of tall green grasses and settles in for a nap.

■ ■ ■

The next day, I text the woman another photo. This one is of their large, wooden bird feeder, which used to hang from a tree branch in the yard and is now on the ground, empty and broken into pieces. I immediately assume that a bear pulled it down and enjoyed a midnight snack of sunflower seeds.

She responds right away: *Bummer. Probably a bear. Better lock the doors at night.*

Me: *Yes, prolly a bear. The dogs sniffed the grass around that area a lot this morning and then tried to sneak out to the road without me.*

Her: *Crap*

■ ■ ■

It's my last day here. Yay! This is a lovely place to hang out, and the animals are sweet and well-behaved—now that we all understand each other—but I have things to do. This house is a twenty-five-minute drive from my condo and fifteen minutes from downtown. I've been doing a lot of driving, sometimes leaving and returning here twice a day for different activities and appointments. As always, there's a limit to how long dogs can hold their pee, and they expect food to be delivered to their bowls at the usual times. So far, fingers crossed, there has been no damage to anything inside the house. The thought of what the leather couches in the living room would look like after a run-in with two sets of German Shepherd teeth makes me scurry back to them as soon as possible. Even though that's unlikely to happen, I am a worrywart. For me, being responsible for other people's houses and their pets is stressful. I should probably re-think this line of work. Stress and anxiety have been a lifelong theme for me. Asking too many questions, proceeding with caution, and double-checking everything is how I navigate most situations—especially when they're unfamiliar.

I'm not sure what time the lady will be back today. I text her a picture of Rocky cocking his head to one side, looking quizzical.

Me: *Do you have an ETA?*

Her: *Today? Or tomorrow?*

What?!!!

Me: *When will I be done staying with Zak and Tia and Rocky?*

Her: *I thought it was tomorrow.*

Me: *Oh. I thought you were returning today. Text above* says, "be back by early afternoon on the 28th."

Which is today. But there's really no reason why I can't stay for another day. I just don't want to. But she's fishing, relaxing, and enjoying herself. And I can use the extra money. I take a deep breath and reply.

Me: *But whatever works for you. I'm not booked tomorrow, so it's no problem for me to stay.* [smiling emoji]

Her: *Ok. I should be there by noon tomorrow.*

■ ■ ■

The next morning, as I'm getting ready to leave, I send her another text—to remind her to let me know when she gets home. I need this closure. I always worry about pets if I don't hear from their people. What if something terrible happens and they don't make it home? In that case, I'll need to return and take care of the pets until an emergency contact person shows up. Sometimes the emergency contact person lives in another town. Or, as in this case, in another state: Colorado. The possibility of the people not making it back home worries my worrywart self every time. I mean, think about it: What if, for whatever reason, the person *never* comes back? Brain freeze!

Who's going to pay me, and when? How do I juggle two critter sitting gigs at once when I have other pets scheduled for the next day, or next week, and they live forty-five minutes apart?

Stop! Everything is fine. Everything is always fine. Deep breath.

At 8:30 a.m. I finish carrying my stuff out to my car, give Zak, Tia, and Rocky some ear scratches, shut them all inside the house, and then drive down the hill, sighing with relief. She paid me on Venmo. I'm done here. Wah-hoo! And it's two days until my next critter sitter gig begins. Lots to do.

■ ■ ■

At 1:35 p.m. I'm standing in a grocery store, trying to decide which bar of dark chocolate to buy, when I suddenly panic. No text. She said she'd be home by noon. The dogs have been alone for more than five hours. I grab my phone.

Me: *Are you home?*

Her: *Yes. Sorry. Since 10:30*

Me: (jaw clenched) *Oh, whew!*

Her: *Sorry!!*

As I often said to my daughter when she was very young and worried about how she looked or what other kids thought of her, "Honey, no one is thinking about you. Ever. They are only thinking about themselves."

True dat.

CHAPTER TEN

Leaving Montana

I've tried to leave Montana many times since my father moved our family to Miles City when I was sixteen years old. At first, I didn't have a specific reason. Well, except maybe for winter, which extends its icy fingers into many of the months officially assigned to fall and spring. I'm not fond of bitterly cold wind and slippery sidewalks. Beyond the hostile weather, however, I soon identified the reality that the Montana of my youth didn't offer many lucrative career choices or jobs. It was not an easy place to make money, and nearly impossible without a college degree or prodigious physical brawn. But perhaps my innate wanderlust would have urged me to leave any place. For me, a career as a photojournalist might have been ideal, but I didn't know anything about that option in the early seventies. And I didn't have any adult guidance or a college fund.

After high school, I intermittently floundered through various jobs: waitress, motel housekeeper, department store clerk, bookkeeper in a bank, insurance secretary, legal secretary. If only I'd thought of working as a critter sitting back then! I hated office work. In fact, I loathed any work that confined me indoors and required me to officially request time off. And I felt itchy for…something.

The summer after I graduated from high school, I took off with a guy named James—not exactly a boyfriend, but we had some chemistry. He may have been auditioning me for the role of his girlfriend. We headed east, hitch-hiking I-94 across North Dakota. Where were we going? Bismarck, at least. Maybe farther. We were just having an open-road, open-plan adventure. Probably my idea. I'm sure I'd imagined spontaneous, freewheeling days filled with fascinating people and places. In reality, we stood on exit ramps under searing summer sun and wandered around filthy truck stops begging people for rides. It took us an entire day to travel a hundred and seventy-five miles. The people we rode with were slightly scary, and not in a fascinating way. It wasn't a fun day. That night, I developed a high fever and a raging sore throat. And I was so tired I could barely stay awake.

James and I huddled inside a metal culvert all night. Poor James. He did his best to keep me from shivering, but I was a hot, sweaty, incoherent mess. The next morning, he wisely decided to get me back home. Pronto.

I don't remember much about the return trip, but I think we rode to Miles City in the cab of a big truck, me in the sleeper. James had walked to the nearest truck stop and found a compassionate long-haul driver with an itinerary that included stops in Glendive and Miles City. James was a good guy, but after we got home I didn't hear from him again for nearly three years, when he and his fiancé asked me to sing at their wedding. Clearly, I had failed the girlfriend audition.

During my two-week hospital stay, while recovering from severe mononucleosis, I decided to enroll in a few classes at Miles Community College—not a high-quality education option, but cheap tuition, and I could live with my parents. I also decided to be done with adventure. A solid life, based on diligent study habits and hard work, was the life for me. But a few months later, I quit school and bought a motorcycle.

A Honda CB175 is not much of a motorcycle. With the throttle wide open on a downhill stretch of road or with a strong tailwind, it maxed out at about sixty miles per hour. At the time, I thought of myself as sort of a badass, riding a real motorcycle. But in fact (I found out years later), the residents of Miles City found me amusing. They saw a tall, lanky, quasi-hippy chick riding a machine that performed a notch or two above a scooter. And yet, I decided to ride that motorcycle more than two thousand miles. Why? Because I could. I didn't know any better and there were no objections from my parents. Why were there no objections from my parents? My dad seemed proud of my moxie. He watched me fasten an olive-green Army Surplus duffle bag to my sissy bar, climb onto my motorcycle, and ride away—maybe wishing he could go, too.

I rode that little bike from Miles City to Salem, Oregon, and back. I left home with seventy dollars in my pocket. The price of gasoline was thirty-five cents a gallon back then, and the Honda averaged seventy-five miles a gallon. Kind relatives and friends gave me places to stay and fed me. After a month, I arrived back in town with fifty-four cents in the front pocket of my 501 Levi jeans.

Once again, the trip wasn't the fun adventure I had imagined. It was lonely out there on the road. A persistent, koan-like question harassed me every day: If no other human shared or witnessed my experiences, did those events actually happen? Without tangible proof—a photograph, a signature in a visitor's log, or a friend to corroborate details—how could I say what was true? Even a paper journal, if I'd kept one, could contain fabrications—according to any other person—and all experience is subjective.

Fiction authors invent entire worlds, believable characters, and astonishing events from the comfort and safety of their writing chairs. That's the nature of fiction. We expect those authors to create stories for our entertainment. But what if some of the stories about my solo adventures didn't happen the way I think they did? There's no one to contradict or verify. Some authors (I'm looking at you, James Frey, and you, Binjamin Wilkomirski) go so far as to fabricate events, stories, and, indeed, entire lives, and then sell them to a gullible public as nonfiction.

So, what should we believe, and why? Perhaps I spent too much time alone, but I began to wonder about reality—that seemingly solid perception of the world that adults had presented to my young, impressionable mind. They wanted me to believe with them, to keep the boundaries of their chosen reality intact. But after my long, solitary trip filled with mind bending questions, I couldn't stay inside their fences. Unwittingly, I had taken something like a hero's journey twenty years before I heard about the archetypal hero from Joseph Campbell.

■ ■ ■

The day after I returned to Miles City, I rode the Honda over a railroad crossing about a block off Main Street. Fortunately, I had slowed to about five miles per hour while looking both ways for trains, because the chain locked up and the bike suddenly skidded to a stop. I managed to keep it upright, drag it to the side of the street, and deploy the kickstand before I dropped down, gasping, to sit cross-legged in the gravel. As I sat there, trying to calm down, I thought: What if the motorcycle's chain had locked up yesterday, or at any other time I'd been traveling at sixty miles per hour on a highway? I would be dead, that's what. My yearning for adventure cooled significantly.

The Honda went into the "For Sale" section of the classifieds in the *Miles City Star*. I tried my best to become a model citizen while experiencing in-state adventures. I took more classes at MCC. I moved to Helena, worked for the Department of Institutions as an accounts receivable clerk, and took classes at Carroll College. I moved to Kalispell and worked in the office of a company that manufactured RVs. I moved to Missoula and worked in the county courthouse, as a "reproduction clerk" (actual job title, not kidding), and as a lackey in the election office. I took classes at the University of Montana. I started my own painting contractor business. What!

Well, why not? The opportunity was there. One of my friends worked as a painter, a skill she'd learned from her father, a professional painting contractor. She gave me a few tips and off I went—again, too ignorant to know what I didn't know. I bid my first job—to apply wood stain to the exterior of a large A-frame cabin—at fifty dollars, plus materials. However, I learned and gained enough experience to take my trade on the road. When the weather turned cold, I headed for California to work for my friend's father.

Each time I moved or got a new job, I was sure it would be the start of my *real* life, and that I'd build a solid foundation from that new life. But disappointment followed each bright new beginning.

From November of 1977 through May of 1978, I lived in the city of Orange. On weekdays, when my boss had enough work for me, I painted houses. Saturdays and Sundays, I worked as a waitress in a little restaurant near Irvine. Southern California delivered great fun for a while—beaches, new friends, new adventures, avocado, grapefruit, lemon, and orange trees in every yard, outdoor concerts.... .

I earned four times more money than I would have made in Montana doing the same work. But I could *see* the air. Standing on the sidewalk in front of the house I shared with two girlfriends on Palmyra Street, I looked down the block and saw an awful brownish-orange color hovering over the neighborhood. It hurt my lungs to breathe that polluted muck. After a few months of commuting through L.A. traffic and choking on smog, I wanted to go home, back to Montana.

After I returned to Helena, I met a man. We lived in Bozeman and then on a ranch near his hometown of Wolf Point. We created the cutest, smartest daughter in the history of the world. We moved back to Bozeman and got a divorce.

In 1991, I tried to leave Montana again. My daughter, Devin, lived with her father's new family in Texas that year, so I decided to drive to Tucson where I had a temporary job lined up. But my car, a used Renault I'd purchased for fifteen hundred dollars, overheated in the desert just north of Page, Arizona. With a car like that, I should have bought a plane ticket to Tucson. Somewhere in the vast network of my brain synapses, however, a strong desire for adventurous road trips made the decisions, even though I hadn't agreed to be dominated by those impulses—not consciously, anyway—and even though none of the road trips I'd ever taken in my entire life had turned out well.

It took the mechanic I found in Page several days to fix my car. Every day, I walked from my cheap motel room to the shop and asked for a progress report. That man probably worked overtime while I was in town, determined to get rid of me as soon as possible.

There wasn't much happening in Page, so I walked to the public library. On a bulletin board in the lobby, I saw a flyer promoting jeep tours in the desert. That sounded fun! I found a pay phone and called the number. It was early April—too late for spring break and too early for summer tourists. The woman with the jeep said she could be available today, immediately. But when she arrived to pick me up, I thought about cancelling. Her leathery skin was pierced and tattooed, not a common sight in the rural West in 1991. She looked like a contestant on a TV wrestling show. But what else would I do during another long day of waiting? Reading was an option, for sure, but I'd been sitting indoors for two days by then. And, after all, I *had* set off on an adventure.

I got into the jeep.

The woman drove me to a place where towers of orange, pink, and red sandstone had tall smooth-walled tunnels running through them. We sat inside those tunnels, on coral-colored sand, and contemplated how long it took water, wind, and time to sculpt rock into monumental works of art. She identified cacti and snakes and birds and lizards for me. She told me stories about herself, the town of Page, and Lake Powell. It was a magical afternoon.

Other than those few hours, however, my days of hanging around Page were long and frustrating. Worse still, once my car was fixed, I had to drive north—through Utah and Idaho and back into Montana. Most of my travel budget had been handed over to the mechanic. In Bozeman, I got on a plane and flew to Tucson for my job, the thing I should have done in the first place.

A couple years later, while trying to find work that paid better than I earned as a personal assistant and from my music gigs, I did some research. What I discovered discouraged me greatly: In the early 1990s, Montana ranked number forty-nine on the list of U.S. states for per capita income. Why am I staying here? I wondered. My determination to find greener financial pastures increased.

I met with a music producer in Los Angeles. He complimented my songwriting. But I really didn't want to live in L.A., even though I loved spending time with my sister, Salli, in Burbank. The smog and traffic hadn't improved much since the Seventies. Also, after a lot of soul searching, I had to admit that I didn't have the necessary ambition: I wasn't willing to do *anything it would take* to be successful in the music business. As a part-time single mother, I needed to try to balance creativity with stability, even though it's impossible.

With that in mind, went to work as a cast driver on movie crews, thanks to Salli's production company and her film industry connections. Off and on for two years, I drove actors—some famous and some not-so-famous—to various locations while working in Texas, South Dakota, Tennessee, and Mississippi. I made good money, but the work was sporadic. When my daughter lived with me, I had to leave her for weeks at a time. I also had to work in the film industry. It sounds glamorous but it's not. My memories of those jobs include many scenes that made me feel uneasy, out-of-place, and insignificant. There was this:

Brett Harrelson sat in the front seat of the SUV I was driving, fidgeting and chattering about a party he and his brother, Woody, had decided to throw at an upscale bar and restaurant.

"All Woody's people will be there," Brett said. Woody's people were his yoga teacher, guitar teacher, personal assistant, girlfriend, and various other members of his entourage who traveled with him. They'd also invited other actors and a few people from the crew.

I pressed the accelerator down, hard, and made it through an intersection just as the light turned to red. "Nice!" Brett shouted. He hated it when I slowed and stopped for yellow lights. He paused mid-fidget, looked over at me. "Do you wanna come?" he asked. "To the party?" But then, quickly, before I could answer, he turned his head toward the passenger-side window and muttered, "No, that probably wouldn't be a good idea."

And this:

Shortly after I parked a Chevy Suburban near the set, located in downtown Memphis, the door on the back passenger's side opened and a production assistant helped Courtney Love climb up onto the seat. She wore heavy makeup and a skimpy dress—her costume for the scene. She looked so thin. The word "skeletal" popped into my mind. She held her right hand aloft, like The Queen poised in mid-wave, an unlit cigarette clamped between her index and middle fingers.

"Can you drive her to the hotel?" the PA asked. I could see the hotel, one block away, but this was my fourth job as a cast driver, so I knew how things were done in the movie business.

"Sure thing," I said, turning the ignition key. The PA shut the door and walked back toward the set. Through the rearview mirror, I saw Courtney look up at me.

"Do you have a light?" she asked, waving her cigarette.

"Yes," I said. I reached up behind me and flicked on the overhead light switch. A thin beam of white light appeared, shining down on Courtney's lap from the roof of the Suburban. I checked for oncoming traffic as I steered out of the parking lot, and then glanced quickly at Courtney in the rearview mirror. The muscles in her face twitched with confusion and then disgust. But she didn't ask again.

I don't know why I flipped on the light. An inability to say "Sorry, but you can't smoke in this vehicle" to a famous person? Sideways sense of humor? But two days later, when I drove Courtney again, she didn't seem to recognize me. Either that, or she didn't care to acknowledge a person too daft to know the difference between an overhead light and a cigarette lighter.

Sometimes the actors in my vehicle ignored me, and sometimes they were friendly and kind: Edward Norton, Frances McDormand, Terry Kinney, Sissy Spacek, Wilford Brimley.

There's also this scenario, which took place during the one time my daughter went on location with me—because she was out of school for the summer.

I stood behind the back wall of the set watching the director of photography peer into a video monitor. Tommy Lee Jones, in his role as director (he was also a principal actor in the film), looked at the monitor, too, as he yelled instructions over the wall to my twelve-year-old daughter, Devin, and a teenaged Blayne Weaver. Devin and Blayne stood outside a screen door that opened onto the set: an ice cream parlor, circa 1906.

"I want you to walk through the door, arm-in-arm," Tommy Lee instructed. "Devin, look at Blayne like you adore him and smile."

I felt anxious about Devin. It was July in West Texas. The temperature was one hundred and seventeen degrees Fahrenheit. She was dressed in a period costume: multiple cotton petticoats under a floor-length heavy white cotton dress with a small bustle, long sleeves, and a high lace collar. She also wore white gloves, long cotton stockings, and black button-up boots. The set was in an old, un-air-conditioned building.

Devin and Blayne linked arms and giggled self-consciously.

Tommy Lee held his hand up in the air for a moment and then brought it down fast. "Action!" he yelled.

Blayne opened the screen door. He and Devin stepped into the ice cream parlor and walked toward one of the white tables.

Tommy Lee yelled "Cut!" He walked around the wall and stood in front of them, laying a hand on his chest. "Blayne, you're courting this young lady" he said. "I want you to be confident, but attentive. "And you need to be a little bit coy," he said, looking at Devin.

Devin and Blayne listened, faces serious, nodding.

"Back to one!" Tommy Lee yelled, striding back behind the wall.

Devin and Blayne walked outside, walked in through the door again, and made it partway across the room before they heard: "Cut!"

More instructions and then another "Action!" and another "Cut!" And again. And again. Then came a second scene. This is how movies are made. It's slow, repetitious, and tedious.

While the grips and electricians made adjustments to the set, Tommy Lee walked around the wall and showed Devin and Blayne what he wanted them to do in the next scene: sit at the table, drink fake ice cream sodas, and pretend to talk. He told Devin to giggle and cover her mouth with her gloved hand. He demonstrated how he wanted them to look at each other. It took about thirty minutes for the set and lighting changes to happen—a short amount of time in the world of movie making. But with each minute that passed, I my worry increased. Devin had been standing in multiple layers of heavy cotton for more than an hour by then, plus the time she'd been in the costume trailer. Visions of heatstroke danced through my mind.

I now understand why stage mothers have their own stereotype. Every cell in my body screeched at me to run over to my daughter, to help her be a perfect character so the scene could end, and she could shed the many layers of clothing before she fainted. But the problem was me, not her. For someone who had never acted before and was on a movie set for the first time, Devin performed brilliantly. And filming multiple takes with multiple cameras at different angles is normal movie-making procedure. The only thing going awry on this set was my anxiety. I should have stayed in my van. Instead, I stood in a dark corner, twisting my fingers and chewing my bottom lip until Devin was escorted back to the wardrobe trailer.

And then there was my job in South Dakota, working on a movie that included several scenes of Crazy Horse and his Oglala Sioux warriors galloping over a hilltop at sunrise. My job included fetching the warriors from their motel rooms at 3 a.m. They all had to get through the costume, hair, and makeup trailers, and onto their horses before dawn. Since a scene that takes place at dawn cannot be filmed at any other time—and the mantra of film executives is "time is money"—all the warriors had to be ready well before sunrise.

Some of the horsemen came outside and got into my van right away after a production assistant made phone calls from the motel office or knocked on their doors. But there were always a few who needed a more physical approach, such as door-pounding, shouts, and threats. Sometimes the PA had to go into the rooms, pull the young men off their beds, propel them out into the parking lot, and shove them through the doors of my van. The smell of that many, unwashed male bodies enclosed in a vehicle after a night on the town is indescribable. I drove with the windows open.

The cast and crew stayed in the town of Hot Springs, which, in 1996, had a population of just over four thousand. In a place that small, there wasn't much for actors and crew members to do during their time off—a boon to the local bars. During the weeks I worked on that movie, my day began between 3 and 5 a.m. and continued until 8 or 9 p.m.—it was a non-union show. Sometimes, I felt as wobbly as the bar-hopping warriors. On the upside, though, I could often read or doze while I waited for my next passengers. To me, sitting in a comfortable van was the best job on the crew. At least I didn't have to ride a horse at breakneck speed down a hill at dawn.

Somehow, though, driving movie people around in vans and SUVs didn't feel like meaningful work. It was boring.

Was I being too picky? Many people would love to make good money driving actors, crew members, or warriors from place to place. They'd love to hang out near movie sets. They'd get to meet famous people, watch how movies are made, and eat free catered gourmet food and snacks from Craft Services. They'd get to work in different locations, explore new cities and rural areas, which I *did* enjoy. The rest? Not so much. What was wrong with me?

The answer to that question might have been that I had no acting ambitions, or that I wasn't a writer trying to get an industry executive to read her screenplay. Or it could have been the constant boredom. So. Much. Boredom. The truth of the situation is that I spent the majority of my working hours sitting around waiting for a call about my next task. I could never venture more than a few feet from my assigned vehicle because an *instantaneous* response to a call from the transportation coordinator was required at all times. On movie sets, a flurry of stressful activity occurs between shots. During that time, everyone scurries around before settling in for the next long wait. The hierarchy bothered me, too, the fact that certain people were considered more privileged than others. And there's so much corporate politics involved in filmmaking, I'm surprised *any* films *ever* get made.

Also, once again, I'd gone off on an adventure that seemed way more fun in my imagination than what I experienced. But driving may have been the perfect job for me. I'm an enthusiastic and persistent driver. After being away from Montana for a few months working on my last movie job, I drove eleven hundred miles in one day, trying to get back to Bozeman by the seventeenth of April, my daughter's birthday. Since then, I've driven more than a thousand miles in one day many times. The distance from Bozeman to my sister's house in Burbank is one thousand and two miles. Sometimes I just can't wait to get there!

■ ■ ■

By the time I returned to live in Southern California in 2017, to take care of Salli's house and her two cats, the air quality had improved. Considerably. It was lovely most of the time. I spent three blessed winters away from Montana's snow and ice. I enjoyed bike rides in February, New Year's Day on the beach, movie theaters where actors and directors appeared onstage for a Q&A after the show, Walt Disney Concert Hall, The Getty, Hollywood Bowl, new musician friends—so many musicians! But I missed my daughter and granddaughters. I missed my other family people and my friends. I missed Montana's wide-open spaces, fresh air, lakes and rivers, camping, and my favorite hiking trails. Los Angeles County offered endless adventures, but it was all unfamiliar territory. Each new experience came with a measure of worry—small or large, depending on the level of uncertainty.

After decades of instability, I've discovered that there's comfort in routines and structure. Life in L.A. required me to reinvent my reality nearly every day. Sometimes, even trips to familiar locations required new routes, depending on traffic conditions. (I laugh when I hear people in Montana call Bozeman "Boz Angeles" in reference to the traffic. Obviously, they've never been to Los Angeles. There's no comparison. The cost of living, however, is now comparable.)

Eventually, as the reality of the pandemic became apparent during March of 2020, I felt a strong urge to be with my own people on familiar ground. Not only that, but many people in Southern California turned hostile during the early days of the shutdown. Unless I wore a mask outside the house, I risked intimidation and nasty remarks. Understandable, perhaps, considering that ten million people are packed into Los Angeles County. But covering my face during a walk to the neighborhood grocery store or while riding my bike felt wrong. So wrong. To me, the outdoors had always been a free and joyful place. Now, it felt scary.

Even inside, though, I experienced a growing dread—fueled by uncertainty and the rising body counts tallied daily and discussed endlessly by experts and media commentators. I finally packed up and drove north. Montana felt safer. And there I could be with most of my best people.

CHAPTER ELEVEN

Jack and Emma: An Unreasonable Schedule

The freezer door is open in the kitchen. The polished wood floor is strewn with bits of Brussels Sprouts and other vegetable debris. WTF? I stand in the kitchen trying to figure out what happened in this house while I was away for four-and-a-half hours.

The freezer compartment is a large slide-out drawer at the bottom of a refrigerator so enormous it looks like it belongs in a restaurant kitchen. I quickly inspect the packages of meat, fruits, and vegetables inside the compartment. Not too soft. Should be fine. I shove the compartment closed and clean up the food scraps on the floor.

I'm not sure how she did it, but there's no doubt about who's responsible for the open freezer: Emma, a ten-year-old arthritic Irish Setter. The other Irish Setter that lives here, a one-year-old named Jack, is not a suspect because I put him in his outdoor kennel before I left. The reason for Emma's mischief is less of a puzzle. She threw a doggy tantrum because lunch was late. Lunch was late for two reasons.

One:

This enormous log house sits near the top of a mountain about thirty minutes east of Bozeman. Half of the drive is over winding, rutted gravel roads where the posted speed limit is twenty miles per hour. There's not much traffic, so I could go faster. But I don't speed because I don't want to damage my small SUV's undercarriage or new tires. The road is poorly maintained. It's so bad, in fact, that the first time I drove up here, to meet the dogs and their people, I nearly quit the job before I arrived. I should have followed that impulse.

Every time I need to go to Bozeman for appointments or errands, to pick up mail or clean clothes at my condo, to play a gig with my band, or to have dinner with friends, I must add at least an hour of driving to the time I can be away from the dogs. Their limit is five hours, which leaves me four hours to accomplish my personal agenda. Plenty of time, yes? No. Being away from this house and these dogs is much more complicated than it seems.

Two:

The dogs have a schedule:

- 5 a.m. wake up
- 6:30 a.m. breakfast

- 11 a.m. morning snack
- 2:30 p.m. lunch
- 4:30 p.m. cocktail hour treats (The dogs eat treats shaped like little weenies and cheesy snacks that look like something from an hors d'oeuvres platter at a human cocktail party.)
- 8 p.m. bedtime

Bedtime is when Jack gets shoved into his nighttime crate— shoved because he doesn't want to get in. Bedtime is when Emma hops up on the bed in the guest room—*my* bed—and flings the quilt around with her paws until it's positioned to her liking before she settles down on it. She then waits for me to occupy the tiny sliver of the queen-sized bed she's left vacant. I'm not ready to go to bed at 8 p.m.! But I must. Because if I don't get in the bed right away, Emma will follow me around the house. If Jack hears her toenails clicking across the floors he will start to bark, and he won't stop until there is no more noise in the house. So, I get under the blankets at 8 p.m. This is a good time to read a book or contemplate why the universe has led me to this particular mountaintop.

For my first two days here, this ridiculous schedule was not a problem. I had twenty oral history interviews to edit, so I brought the equipment I needed for work. I also brought a portable wi-fi device and jump drives to back up my files. The Internet service here is crap. It comes from a satellite dish. When the wind blows, the Internet connection blows away, too, so I can't count on backing up my files in Dropbox.

Unfortunately, the cell service is also crap. The only place in the house my phone gets a signal is on the northwest side of the wrap-around deck. It's about twenty-five feet off the ground and has a clear view of the Bridger Mountains, where there must be a cell tower. Yesterday, I had to redial a client twice because I forgot not to walk around. I'm not used to sitting still during phone conversations. I wear a headset and can often log a couple of thousand steps on my Garmin while I listen and respond.

But anyway, there are no gaps in the eating schedule for these dogs that would allow me to be away for long. Although I'd done my best to manage their foody expectations today, I *had* to be gone for several hours. My band played a gig at a local retirement community, and the process of setting up and playing took more than three hours. Add in an hour of driving time, plus a quick stop at the grocery store, and my allotted five hours were nearly gone. I needed things from my condo, but I didn't dare risk the extra thirty minutes it would have taken to add that task to my itinerary.

I left the house shortly after giving the dogs their 11:30 a.m. snack and returned at 4 o'clock, ninety minutes past lunch time. And so, Emma opened the freezer. Since she didn't take anything out—apparently not hungry enough to gnaw on a frozen T-bone—I assume she intended to send me a message about my failure to perform critter sitter duties to her satisfaction.

The kitchen scraps scattered across the floor were mostly citrus rinds and the trimmings from root vegetables. I guess she's not fond of sweet potatoes, beets, or carrots. My bad for leaving those in a plastic bag sitting in the sink. In my defense, there's no place to get rid of kitchen scraps on this property. Any food item left outside, or in the garage, will attract bears, who will rip doors off garages to get at the contents of trash containers stored inside. I've seen the damage done to garage doors by hungry bears with my own eyes, so I'm not taking any chances. Kitchen scraps must be driven down the mountain, on the terrible, rutted gravel road, and put into one of the locked, bearproof collection bins by I-90. Obviously, I didn't do that when I drove down the mountain today. I was focused on the band gig, on checking to be sure I had all my instruments and equipment with me.

As I said, Emma was the only dog free to roam the house while I was away. Her "brother" (as the people call Jack) was in his outdoor kennel—one of three options I have available for containing his exuberant Irish Setter energy. The other two options are large metal crates. His daytime crate is under the open stairway in the TV and exercise room located on the lower level of the house—a huge room with floor to ceiling windows and spectacular views of the Bridger Mountains. Jack's nighttime crate is in the two-car garage attached to the house, which is mostly empty, except for another large refrigerator/freezer, several cases of soda stacked against a wall, and a recycling container.

The building where the people park their vehicles is an oversized three-car combination garage and workshop that sits across the gravel driveway about thirty feet from the house. Why seventy-something people would choose to walk across snow and ice in the winter to get to their house, when they could drive into a heated garage attached to their log mansion, is way too much for my brain to comprehend. Not my business. But, as a critter sitter, the open freezer in the kitchen *is* my business. The next time I leave the house, I'll put a barricade in front of it.

I've have taken care of these dogs before. The first time, though, I only stayed with them for five days. I treated that gig as a mini-vacay and only made one quick trip into town. Except for Jack's jumping and barking, we got along fine—maybe because I served all their meals and snacks at the proper time. This two-week stay, however, is proving to be more of a challenge.

I give Emma my evilest evil eye as I pass her on my way to the front door to let Jack in, so he'll stop barking. She stares back at me, cool and aloof, from the leather chair where she's lounging. Jack barrels through the door, nearly knocking me over. He races to Emma, sniffs her for half a second, and then runs back to jump on me. His toenails stab into my shoulder blades when I turn my back on him.

"Off!" I yell.

Jack doesn't care about my command, but since his attention doesn't stay on anything for long, he soon bounds away to grab one of his toys. But then, through the window, he spots a red-tailed chipmunk on the trunk of a pine tree next to the free-standing garage. He drops his toy. He sprints across the living room and leaps onto a wooden bench under the window—placed there on purpose as a dog perch, I'm guessing—and the barking begins again. Inside this time. At an ear-splitting volume. Emma jumps out of the chair and starts barking, too—with astonishing ferocity.

"Come on you guys," I yell through the cacophony, "it's a chipmunk!" Good grief. I can't imagine how they'll react if a real threat appears.

Jack leaps off the bench and then onto it again—down and up and down and up and down and up—while barking non-stop. I marvel at his energy and coordination. He runs over to the front door and jumps against it, standing on his hind legs while frantically scratching at the wood with his front paws. It's an expensive, hand-made door, but I'm not concerned about the damage. The day I came here for my interview, I noticed that the door was already well gouged. Another sign of things to come I chose to ignore.

I shove Jack away from the front door and flip the deadbolt. The people told me to keep the door locked with the deadbolt because Jack knows how to open it. This is true. The door has a lever handle that unlatches when you push down on it. Easy peasy for Jack. The day I arrived, I forgot to lock the door after he came inside. A few minutes later, from the other side of the house, I heard distant barking and ran into the living room. The door was wide open, and Jack was outside, running amok.

I try to pull the front door open in between Jack's leaps, throwing my elbow into his chest each time he launches his body toward me and the door. It is an athletic event worthy of an entry in any exercise journal. Pulling the front door open is only one of many dog-related athletic events I participate in during my time at this house. There's ball throwing, wrestling Jack into his crates, getting up to open the door for him to go out and in fifty times each day, jogging around the property while trying to convince him to come back inside when he's barking at 5:15 a.m. (there are neighbors and, even though they're not close by, sounds travel far out here). My attempts to put a positive spin on this free exercise regimen are about forty percent successful. Sometimes.

Eventually, I'm able to pull the door open, and both dogs run out into the gravel driveway with chipmunk murder in their hearts. I step out onto the wide deck that wraps around the front half of the house and focus on the warmth of the late afternoon sunshine and the gorgeous mountain views. Ahhh... it really is a wonderful place to be. Well, except for the dogs.

■ ■ ■

When Ann from Ohio visits, I find a way to be with my friends, despite my restrictive dog duties. It seems easiest to invite Ann, Shan, and Shan's sister, Lynne, to have lunch with me here, so I won't have to worry about being away from the dogs for too long. I know my friends will enjoy spending a few hours in this beautiful place. And they'll be able to deal with Emma and Jack because they're all dog lovers with dogs of their own.

Before they arrive, I spend the morning throwing balls for Jack, trying to wear him out so he won't jump on everyone. An unrealistic goal, I know, but I'm hoping he'll have less energy for jumping.

Jack and I are out in the driveway when my friends arrive. He bounds over to Lynne's SUV and enthusiastically greets each woman as she steps out onto the gravel. They all pat his head as he sniffs them and wiggles with excitement.

"Come on, Jack," I yell from the front porch. He bolts away from Ann and runs a wide lap around the perimeter of the driveway. "Jack. Come." He's about to lunge at Shan when I press a button on his training collar. It buzzes against his neck. He skids to a stop and looks over at me. "Come," I say again. He lopes over to the porch and trots through the front door as I hold it open. Once he's inside, I shut the door and turn back to my friends. Jack immediately starts scratching at the door and barking. I wave my friends to the porch and tell them to wait ten seconds before coming in.

Inside the house, I straddle Jack, pressing my knees into his ribs while the three women come through the door. He bucks and tries to get at them while I hold him back by grabbing the two collars around his neck (invisible boundary fence collar and training collar). Once they're inside, I shove him back outside to give my friends a chance to look around, choose a beverage, and find a comfortable chair. While we hug, chatter, and comment on the house and the stunning mountain views, Jack runs from one side of the deck to the other, barking, whining, and raking his claws across all the living and dining room windows.

Meanwhile, Emma offers herself to everyone for admiration and petting, taking advantage of the rare opportunity to get to visitors before Jack does. There's no hint of the devious, devil dog who opens the freezer, scatters kitchen scraps, and hides books and car keys under her dog bed (yes, she did that, too). No Irish Settler on the planet is as well-behaved and angelic as Emma is right now. I think she knows exactly what she's doing: showing everyone what a wonderful dog she is, compared to Jack, the bad dog frantically leaping, barking, and crying on the other side of the windows.

My friends can see what they're in for when Jack comes inside, but I must let him in or he'll continue his assault on the windows, and our ears. I put our lunch on the table and invite everyone to sit, hoping the dining room table will create a partial protection barrier for them. We brace ourselves for Jack's high-energy entrance.

"Throw your elbows out and turn away if he jumps at you," I say.

After I open the door, I step in front of Jack to make sure he sees the training collar remote in my hand. He understands what that is.

"You be a good boy," I say, pointing the remote at him. "No jumping. NO jumping." Jack doesn't like getting shocked, of course. He prances and quivers until I step aside. And then, he runs full speed across the great room, aiming at the dining room table. I press the buzzer on the remote, a warning. He slows.

When he reaches the table, Jack remembers to stay off our guests for a few seconds. He greets Ann and Shan with enthusiastic snuffles and short jumps that remind me of prancing Lipizzaner horses. But when he gets to Lynne, he can't contain himself. He jumps at her face. I press the shock button. He yips and careens sideways.

For about ten seconds, Jack stands completely still, legs wide apart. His feathery red tail is erect, but not a hair on it moves. He looks at me with accusatory and mournful eyes. I feel terrible, but now he knows what I expect of him. He's a very smart dog. And forgiving. When I sit down at the table, he comes over and leans against me.

We eat lunch with Emma lying under the table and Jack circling us—until he spots something moving outside. He runs to one of the windows and starts barking. I let him out and, in, several times, while we eat.

"It's good exercise," I tell my friends cheerfully.

Jack's trips outside are short because he wants so much to be with the people inside his house. Irish Setters are notorious for their devotion to family and their enthusiasm for new friends. People love these rambunctious red dogs, and these dogs love people—maybe a little too much. Their joyful energy is part of the Irish Setter package. Jack is a high-spirited, playful gun dog, a classic example of his breed. I can tell he wants to be good, but he has trouble containing his energy. All I can do is try to stay uninjured until his people return. My job is to work with what's here. I can't correct Jack's bad habits, so I don't even try.

We eat lunch, enjoy the view, and chat while petting Irish Setters. Emma and Jack are thrilled to have visitors and I'm thrilled to have time with my friends. We give as much love and attention as we can to these dogs that (I imagine) are missing their people.

CHAPTER TWELVE

No Hiking Trails

Here I am, living on the side of a mountain with Jack and Emma for two weeks, surrounded by forested land that looks like it should have at least *one* hiking trail running through it. But there are no hiking trails. Every bit of the land is privately owned. It's a vertical subdivision with flat building sites carved into it. Maybe this mountain was sold off by the U.S. Forest Service after it extracted all the money it could from timber sales. This is my assumption because USFS is responsible for National Forest lands and it's the government agency that usually owns mountainsides. Or it might have been owned by the Bureau of Land Management, a U.S. Department of Interior agency that "manages one in every 10 acres of land in the United States." Either way, the land, formerly *our* land, is sold to the highest bidder. And then we, the tax-paying people, no longer have access to some of our favorite areas to hike and camp —no access to our land because it's no longer our land, even though we've had access to it for as long as we can remember.

The new owners build huge houses and cut off public access to their private property. Of course, capitalism automatically grants them that right. They paid for the land. They own it. But then people like me, who used to take my daughter camping near a certain trailhead a few miles north of Bozeman, arrive one Friday afternoon to find a fancy metal gate blocking the access road.

And speaking of access roads: When I played guitar and sang in the band *The VooDoo Hot Dogs with Sweet Relish*, we once booked a gig at an enormous house on a mountain top in the Bridgers. The people who hired us fed sixty people, plus our band, at a sit-down dinner in their living room, with plenty of space to spare. We set up our equipment on their stone terrace, which, of course, had a killer view. All eight of us and our gear fit on one end of the stone terrace, leaving plenty of room for dancing. The owner of the house—a man who looked like a middle-aged model for GQ magazine—told me it cost a million dollars to build the road from the county highway up the side of the mountain to their house. And that was in 2002. I can't imagine what it would currently cost—if they could even find an available contractor with the time to build it.

This price tag was incomprehensible to me then, and it's not any easier for me to comprehend now. The inequitable distribution of wealth in the world bothers me, even though I'm glad I live in the United States, a capitalist country. I'm smart and hardworking, but obviously I've focused on the wrong types of work all my life. Music, writing, and audio production are rarely lucrative, and yet I have never been able to stop myself from making those choices. Doing any other work has always felt completely wrong to me. For decades, I tried and failed to be interested in other careers.

During the 1990s, when Bozeman real estate went crazy, a realtor friend encouraged me to get my license and jump into the bedlam. My parents also suggested the same thing, more than once. But every cell in my body shuddered at the thought of making that choice. I was deep into my singer/songwriter experience. I wondered how paperwork, office hours, marketing, and appointments with sellers and buyers would fit into unanticipated bursts of creativity, and my out-of-town gigs. That conundrum has appeared many times during my adult life. A boyfriend once asked me to move in with him. He said he'd pay all my living expenses. I only had to keep the house clean and cook dinner for him.

"But what if I'm in the middle of writing a song at 4:30 and you want dinner at 6 o'clock?" I asked him.

"Well, then," he replied, "we'd have a problem."

This man claimed to love me *and* my creativity, but he wanted me to be creative on a schedule. Can creativity be scheduled? I guess I didn't love him enough, either.

Instead of striking off into a lucrative real estate career while the proverbial iron was hot, I took critter sitter jobs, which I thought gave me more creative freedom and flexibility. I didn't consider the long-term financial, emotional, physical instability of this choice because I didn't know any better. I looked for a way to pay my bills *and* do the work I loved. Many best-selling authors offered advice and encouragement.

Susan Jeffers told me to "feel the fear and do it anyway." Joseph Campbell persuaded me to "follow my bliss." Shirley MacLaine beckoned me toward the light. Deepak Chopra and Wayne Dyer assured me I could manifest anything my heart desired. I diligently followed their instructions. I wanted to believe in the magic, to be a shining example of personal power, of the human ability to surmount the insurmountable. In my case, to gain financial independence.

But nothing turned out the way I imagined. And now it's too late for me to make different decisions—to take the road more traveled. There aren't enough years left in my lifespan for me to benefit much from compound interest. Applying for jobs is now more difficult. Local employers try, without success, to hide their shock when my wrinkled face shows up for an interview. By law, government agencies are not allowed to discriminate based on age, but (in my experience) their online applications always require a date of birth. Since 2020, when the pandemic decimated my freelance career, I've submitted dozens of applications without a single interview invitation.

What if I had made different decisions when I was younger? What if, instead of moving in and out of other people's houses—some of whom can afford to pay millions of dollars for a driveway—I'd worked for thirty or forty years at a job with benefits? I give myself a minute to feel sorry for myself, even though I know it's pointless, a waste of my time and energy.

But then I remember the issue of wildfires, and I have to calm myself down again.

Should I, who can't afford a house in my hometown, and can no longer hike or camp in some of the nearby forests because they're privately owned, be required to pay for protecting the ginormous houses wealthy people have built there? This question comes up every summer during wildfire season. Why should the rest of us have to pay to save those homes? Solutions to those contentious issues might currently be grinding their way through some lawsuit or government bureaucracy. But right now, all I know is that there's nowhere for me to walk myself or Jack on this privately-owned mountain.

The option of taking Jack for a walk along the rutted gravel road presents several problems. First, I'd have to remove his invisible boundary fence collar and use the training collar, which worries me. He's fast. He can probably sprint from zero to beyond the collar's range before I can get the remote into position and press the button. While I don't know for sure that that's true, potential dangers lurk everywhere along the road: other people's property (Montana is a Stand Your Ground state), other dogs, mama bears with cubs, work trucks speeding around corners... .

Clipping Jack to a leash and walking him on the road is not a good option, either. I know I'm not strong enough to control him when he lunges at a squirrel, or whatever else catches his attention. And so, I must settle for burning off his excess energy by throwing balls and toys for him to chase on this property.

For me—a lover of forests and a hiker since childhood—
living on a mountain with no hiking trails is a completely
mind-bending situation. Every day, several times a day, I look
outside and automatically think about going for a walk. To
heck with Jack. *I* need time in the forest. I need time for my
own exercise. But then I remember that I'd have to drive at
least forty-five minutes from here to get to a trail where we,
the people, still have access. So, for today, my cardio workout
option is downstairs, where there's an elliptical machine.

CHAPTER THIRTEEN

Jack and Emma: Seeing Stars

Jack watches me from his crate under the stairway, waiting as patiently as he can, which is not very patiently. He fidgets and whines. I feel sorry for him, but I can't let him run around the house while I'm on the elliptical machine. He would bark and jump at the windows, and I wouldn't be able to see what other mischief he was up to. Yesterday, while I was in the kitchen chopping vegetables, he shredded one corner of his dog bed. He pulled most of the stuffing out, leaving a blizzard of white polyester strewn across the floor of the living room. I can't seem to anticipate, or prepare for, or avoid, what these dogs decide to do. They require a great deal of my attention. By mid-afternoon each day, my head aches from the constant vigilance.

Most people believe that hanging out with other people's pets is a nice, easy gig. And sometimes it is. But mostly it isn't. Not for me, anyway. While a sweaty cardio workout helps somewhat with stress relief, this house and these dogs constantly poke at my innate anxieties. I hope Emma is behaving herself upstairs.

When I let Jack out of his crate after my workout, he goes crazy. Again. He runs up and down the entire stairway three times before my feet are on the fifth step. He throws his body against mine while I climb. I hang onto the metal rail and try to push him away. He won't stop, no matter what I say. Yelling doesn't deter him—it just hurts my vocal cords. So, I clamp my mouth shut and concentrate on staying upright, carefully placing my feet on each step. It occurs to me, much too late, that I should have brought the training collar's remote downstairs. Another lesson learned. How do the people who live here, both in their seventies, avoid getting knocked down by this dog?

I must not get injured. There's no cell phone service from the lower level of this house, even though there are huge windows spread across one of the walls. So even if I'm still conscious after falling down the stairs, I won't be able to call 911.

We make it up to the living room where Jack alternates between slamming his body against me and crashing into the front door as I'm trying to open it to let him outside. If only I had the presence of mind to remember that Jack can open the door himself, after I unbolt it, this would be easy. But in this moment, with all the body slamming and barking, and late-afternoon mind fatigue, I've forgotten he has that skill.

Once I can finally open the wooden door and the storm door, and Jack runs outside, I grab a few toys and balls from a basket.

"Hey, Emma," I say. "Let's go outside."

Emma raises her head, looks at me for a few seconds, and then eases herself out of the chair. We squeeze ourselves through the doors between Jack's leaps against them from the outside.

A sliding glass door in the dining room leads to the wrap-around deck. After we're all outside, I realize that would have been an easier exit for Emma and me. But I never let Jack out that door because I'm afraid he will crash straight through the screen door behind it before I can slide it open. I don't want to explain a ripped screen door to Jack's people. I try to return people's houses to them in the same condition they're in when I arrive. That includes cleaning. In this case, I know I have at least an hour of window washing to do, inside and out, to remove all the doggy drool and nose grease from the hundreds of square feet of windows in the living and dining rooms. The people who live here must wash windows every day! But I only intend to do it once. That's a task for the last day.

When I've managed to get myself and Emma out onto the covered front porch, she saunters over to the nearest water bowl. There are four water bowls outside. It's part of my job to refill them all twice each day. While Emma laps water, I walk across the broad front porch and out onto the driveway. It's only a few feet but it's not easy. While I'm on the porch, Jack leaps up on me. He jumps up at least once for each step I take. He can't wait for the games to begin.

Again, why don't I have the training collar remote in my hand? Some lessons take a long time to learn.

Honestly, though, I admire Jack's energy, tenacity, and speed. Every time he jumps on me, I stiff-arm him in the chest, but he does not get discouraged. He falls backward for a split second, rights himself, and then leaps at me again. And again and again and again... .

Jack is just over a year old, and his energy is endless. I wonder about the wisdom of oldsters adopting an Irish Setter puppy—a *male* Irish Setter puppy. This is another of their choices that I don't understand. But again: not my business. My business right now is staying alive and uninjured for the next twelve days. I probably shouldn't take care of these dogs anymore. It doesn't feel safe for me. Too bad, though. The rate of pay is above average. The view is gorgeous. And, except for the barking, it's peaceful and quiet.

Out in the wide gravel driveway, my serious upper-body workout begins.

When a bulldozer leveled an acre, or so, of the mountain to create a building site, it left a steep hill on one side of the driveway. This is Jack's exercise hill. I haven't tried to count how many times he runs up and down it in a day, but it's probably in the hundreds. Emma walks up the hill twice: early morning and late evening. I throw the ball uphill for about ten minutes, alternating my arms until they're both tired. It's time to change directions.

The other side of the driveway slopes steeply downhill. It's beautifully landscaped with native grasses, flowering bushes, gravel pathways, and wide flagstone steps that wind down to a firepit surrounded by large stones and Adirondack chairs. I walk across the driveway and see Emma ambling along the gravel path just above the firepit. Jack follows me, waiting for our game of fetch to resume. I pause, arm raised, relishing this brief hiatus from his constant movement. When I see that he can't wait any longer, I hurl a large orange nylon chew stick toward the fire pit. It doesn't quite get there. My arms feel rubbery. On his way to find it, Jack gets distracted and takes his time. He wends and snuffles a zig-zag pathway through stands of vegetation. During this break in the action, I have an idea.

Jack's toys are scattered everywhere on this property. His people told me not to worry about collecting them, and I haven't. But now I hunt through the spikey grasses and flowering bushes until I find a splintered bone with bits of marrow clinging to the inside—once part of a slaughterhouse animal, no doubt. This might be a prize that'll hold Jack's attention. He lopes uphill toward me. I point toward a cluster of Aspen and pine trees standing near the detached garage, where a dense thicket of bushes surrounds the tree trunks.

"Over there," I say to Jack, making sure he sees where I point.

I fling the bone as far as my exhausted arm can manage. It lands somewhere inside the tangle of branches and leaves. Jack sprints down the hill and into the bushes. I'll have to pick bits of stickery plants out of his long, red hair later, but at this moment I don't care. I need a break from that high-energy dog.

"Hey, Emma," I call softly, not wanting to deter Jack from his brushy quest. She lifts her head and ambles over to me. We sit, Emma on the gravel path in front of a rosehip bush, me on a huge rock embedded in soil next to the path. I scratch her head. We watch clouds float over the peaks of the Bridger Mountains. We listen to the crack of branches and the rustle of leaves as Jack plows around the thicket searching for the bone. We enjoy the moment.

■ ■ ■

It's late afternoon. I walk outside, curious about why Jack isn't standing on the front porch whining to be let in. He's been outside for about fifteen minutes. Normally, he'd be scratching on the door or barking by now. Silence is *not* golden when it's connected to an energetic Irish Setter. I walk the perimeter of the house, calling his name. Jack does not appear. Uh, oh.

The area of this property where the dogs are allowed to roam is inside an invisible fence. Whenever the dogs get close to the boundary, their collars beep. If they cross the boundary, the collars deliver a jolt of electricity. During my interview/ orientation (the people hired me five minutes after I arrived), the man assured me that the boundary fence is a fail-safe way to keep Emma and Jack contained. But something has obviously gone wrong.

I hurry back inside the house and grab the remote for Jack's training collar. I walk around the house again, pressing the button, yelling his name. When he doesn't yelp, I know he's far away, beyond the invisible fence boundary. I run up the driveway and out onto the road. I look to my right and see him trotting up the dirt road that leads to the top of the mountain. He's just about to go around a corner—out of my sight and deeper into black bear and mountain lion territory.

"Jack," I shout. He stops and looks back. I press the buzz button. He doesn't flinch. He's too far away. "Hey, where's your ball!" I yell, swinging my arms and jumping around. He considers this option for a moment. He *does* love to play. But on the other hand…he turns to look back up the road.

During his moment of indecision, I pull my phone out of my pocket, zoom in to 10x with the camera app, and take a picture of Jack standing far beyond his people's property. Luckily, my phone has bars in this uphill spot. I send the picture and a text message to the woman.

Me: *Jack is out on the road!*

While I wait for a reply, Jack finishes considering my offer of play time and makes the right decision. He trots down the road toward me. But he doesn't run flat out, as usual. He holds back, as if he might still change his mind. It may have been a tough decision for him, but I think his innate love of people and play time appealed to him more than a solitary exploration of the great unknown waiting at the end of the road. My phone dings.

Her: *Oh dear! The battery probably needs to be replaced. In the treat cabinet there is a maroon bag on the upper shelf with extra batteries for his fence collar. You can test it after you put in the new battery by going into garage and holding the collar near invisible fence box. Be careful not to allow prongs near you or you will be shocked!*

WTH! Which garage? Nothing about invisible fence boundary maintenance was included in my orientation or on the pages of written instructions for taking care of Jack and Emma. I have a better idea.

I coax Jack inside the house, where Emma is napping in her usual leather armchair. Jack whines and barks while I wrestle with him, trying to unfasten his invisible fence collar so I can replace it with Emma's collar.

"Hold still!" I say, but he wriggles harder. He wants the ball-throwing session I promised him. Now. When I finally get his collar off, I walk over to Emma. But she is not wearing a collar. Where is her collar?

I grab my phone while Jack paces and whines.

Me: *Emma doesn't have a collar on!*

Her: *Emma's green invisible fence collar is hanging with the leashes by the front door.*

Emma is ten years old, stiff and rickety. But they didn't tell me she wasn't wearing the collar anymore. The last time I stayed with these dogs, they both had invisible fence collars on their necks. It's now 7:30 p.m. Almost bedtime. I'm tired of wrestling with Jack. I decide to deal with all this tomorrow morning. I put Jack's training collar remote into my pocket, and we go outside for a short game of fetch.

■ ■ ■

Early the next morning, I discover that the battery in Emma's collar is also dead. So, I replace the battery in Jack's collar, but it doesn't work. He runs right past the boundary to the road and starts up the mountain again. I call him back with treats and text the woman to give her an update. She replies, *When he is out, the training collar with the remote would be your best bet.*

Terrific. I'll have to be with him whenever he's outside. It's going to be a difficult day. But my stay here is almost over. The people's flight is scheduled to arrive at Bozeman airport tomorrow at noon. Hallelujah! Oh, dear God, please don't let it be cancelled or late.

Later, after I give up trying to work, because Jack keeps barking and wanting me to let him in and out, I grab a few toys out of the basket. In the driveway, Jack prances and leaps, waiting for me to throw a ball for him to chase up the steep hill. My first underhanded toss falls short of the top. The ball rolls down and skitters across the gravel toward my feet. Jack circles me, barking with joy. I ignore the pain in my arm and try again. This time the ball lands on top of the hill.

Jack sprints up the steep incline and grabs it with his teeth. But then, he suddenly drops the ball, distracted by an irresistible smell near a small pine tree. The ball rolls down the hill. I pick it up and wait for him to return to our game, but he's forgotten about me. He paws at the soil, focused completely on whatever is under the ground near that tree. Yay! I walk over to the front porch and sit down in one of the red Adirondack chairs.

It's hot outside, and it feels good to sit in the shade. I lean my head against the chair and close my eyes. I love how quiet it is on this mountain. The nearest house, which I know is there, but can't see, is mostly unoccupied. I've been told it's a vacation home for a family that lives back east. That house is huge, gabled, and painted yellow with white trim. It looks like it belongs on a cliff above the Atlantic Ocean. Emma's and Jack's people told me the owners have family gatherings there once or twice a year.

A familiar sting invades my solar plexus as I try to imagine what it would feel like to have so much money that I could afford to leave a big house unoccupied for more than ten months a year while paying for utilities, maintenance, and a caretaker. Can I even imagine? Probably not with any accuracy. How did this happen to me, I wonder for the billionth time? How is it possible that I'm working as a pet sitter in my late sixties? Or working at anything? I sigh and force my attention back to the present moment.

A few minutes later, I open my eyes and turn my head to look up at the spot where I last saw Jack. He's not there. Oh, no! I forgot about the malfunctioning invisible fence collar.

I leap out of the chair and start yelling, "JACK! JACK!"

Magically, Jack appears at the top of the hill. He strikes a regal sideways pose and gazes down at me. He looks magnificent, like a glossy red-haired canine prince waving his tail feathers. He is Irish Setter perfection. I am enchanted by his beauty and *joie de vivre*.

Suddenly, he races down the hill with blazing speed and leaps on me before I can step aside. My tail bone slams into the deck. The back of my head smashes into one of the huge logs on the side of the house, and I see stars—at 10:30 a.m.

CHAPTER FOURTEEN

Main Street to The Mountains

Thirty-five years ago, when I owned in a house on South Church Avenue in Bozeman, the north end of Burke Park was a still a scrap of hillside pasture called Peet's Hill. My house sat directly across the street from the pasture, which was populated at the time by a lone horse. A narrow footpath wound through the horse's field and up the hill. My house was also one block from the Gallagator Trail, an old railroad line that's part of the Rails-to-Trails system. I could open my front door and walk for miles after crossing only one street.

Peet's Hill was a popular place to sled in winter. From my living room window, I watched mobs of teenagers cling to a old mattress as they careened down the slope, screaming and bouncing off into the snow. Children on saucers and wooden sleds with metal runners shot across the snow while their parents stood at the bottom of the hill to be sure they didn't hit the barbed wire fence, or slide under it and out onto the street.

In those days, Peet's Hill was private property, but local people were allowed to walk and sled on it. I walked there during the spring, summer, and fall seasons. I'd cross the street and duck through the strands of barbed wire fence, careful not to snag my clothes on the pointy metal prongs. Inside the pasture, I'd follow the narrow path trampled into the soil by the horse's hooves, which zigzagged up from the seasonal creek to the top of the hill. As I walked, I collected sprigs of fragrant sage and red-orange rose hip berries. These days, such harvesting is discouraged, which makes sense. If all people who walk there now picked sage or rose hips, the land would be stripped bare within a few weeks. Back then, though, things were different.

Bozeman was a small town of about seventeen-thousand people in the mid-1980s. Whenever I walked up the hill, I rarely saw anyone else, except sometimes on weekends. Now, I encounter herds of people and dogs every day of the week. And it's rare to see anyone walking or jogging the Burke Park/ Peets Hill trails without a dog. Sometimes, I'll see one person with four or five dogs.

Now that Peet's Hill is part of Burke Park, there are many trails, benches, and dog poop collection bins. The place is constantly used from dawn to dusk, seven days a week. I mean, who wouldn't want to walk there? The views of the Gallatin Valley are magnificent from the top of the hill. The trails are wide and well-maintained. The sunsets are spectacular.

The people of Bozeman have the late Chris Boyd to thank for this beautiful park. Chris was a musician, environmental activist, and visionary. In 1990, he founded the Gallatin Valley Land Trust (GVLT) and worked tirelessly to negotiate the purchase of land that became Burke Park and Peet's Hill. Thanks to Chris, GVLT operates with a mission "to conserve open space on a scale that maintains the agricultural heritage, healthy and abundant wildlife habitats, clean flowing waters, and the scenic beauty of Montana's greater Yellowstone region, now and for all future generations, while also developing extensive trail systems that connect communities to their surrounding natural lands and to each other." Whew! That's an ambitious mission. And one, I imagine, that's become increasingly difficult to achieve in the wake of our latest influx of new residents. The staff at GVLT must be working at breakneck speed, trying to make deals with landowners before developers swoop in with cash. It must be challenging.

Since I love walking trails, it's a joy to donate money to GVLT. Without the diligence of Chris, GVLT staff, and another visionary named Don Weaver (who developed the Sourdough Trail system), the Gallatin Valley would have far fewer trails, open spaces, and protected land. As it turned out, Chris's vision was timely.

During the summer of 1991, while the movie *A River Runs Through It* was being filmed in the area, crew members from Los Angeles gawked at the low prices of houses in Bozeman and Livingston. They started buying real estate and re-selling it to their friends in L.A. for double and triple the money. Once the movie was released in theaters in 1992, and people saw Montana's beautiful rivers and scenery on big screens, tourism boomed. Fly fishing and owning property in Montana became a status symbol. Demand for houses and land in the Bozeman area rose, and prices skyrocketed.

The new buyers—including powerful, wealthy men from the media and entertainment industries—all wanted the same thing: acreage with trees and a creek running through it (if an entire river wasn't available). Realtors and building contractors prospered. Attorneys prospered, as well, because the new owners wanted privacy and legal dominion over their land and (what they considered to be their) water. Legal battles turned especially bitter when wealthy landowners tried to stop the locals from fishing in "their" water. Fights over access rights escalated in county and state courtrooms and dragged on for years. State legislators scrambled to present bills that would defend citizens' rights in traditional ways. New environmental nonprofits were created to protect Montana's land and water, and their attorneys joined the fray. Other attorneys filed lawsuits on behalf of well-established environmental and sportsman nonprofit organizations.

Battles over land and water have been fought in Montana since the early 1800s. After the Louisiana Purchase, the Corps of Discovery ventured west in 1803. Once the territory was mapped, the U.S. government offered free land to intrepid pioneers. The native people, who were already living and hunting on this land, were slaughtered and forced onto reservations. Whenever they left the reservation looking for animals to feed their families, they were murdered by U.S. soldiers or settlers—because it was legal (and considered heroic) to do that in the 1800s. Although modern battles are fought in courtrooms, they are still intense.

Conflicts over Montana's land and water escalated sharply in the 1990s after a media billionaire and a rock star both filed lawsuits to protect their rights as property owners. The media billionaire's lawsuit, which aimed to prevent local people from accessing the Ruby River, prompted defensive action by Trout Unlimited. TU claimed the lawsuit was just one in a series of attempts to overturn Montana's stream access law. The stream access law guarantees anglers and recreationists the right to access public waters by staying within the ordinary high-water mark of rivers and streams. The definition of "public waters" raged on while the rock star's experts claimed "harm to a fishery" if the public had access to "his" water, which flowed within a public, man-made ditch.

Was it public or private water? The laws are complicated. The rock star's case failed when Montana's Supreme Court decided in favor of the public. The billionaire's battle to control access to a county bridge and access to the river went on for more than twelve years. It finally petered out after an appeal deadline passed without any further action by the landowner's attorneys. I'm sure everyone involved was exhausted by then. The way I saw the story unfold, it looked like the billionaire and his legion of well-paid lawyers were defeated by a gang of guerrilla-style volunteers. Something about rich guys trying to block access to public water made Montanans go ballistic.

Citizen action groups have deep roots in this state, beginning with the vigilantes who punished criminals in the gold rush settlements long before paid law enforcement officials arrived. The amount of time and money spent on legal battles over private land and water issues in recent history is staggering. But other legal processes benefit everyone.

Thanks to GVLT's efforts to "conserve open space" (i.e., buy land), Peet's Hill, Burke Park, Gallagator Trail, Sourdough Trail, and others, are all part of a one-hundred-mile trail system called Main Street to the Mountains. In Bozeman, we can stroll, hike, jog, bike, push baby strollers, or cross-country ski until we drop. Even though the quality of life has diminished with all the new people moving in so rapidly, it's still a pretty darn good place to live.

My quality of life would be a lot better, however, if I still owned that house on South Church Avenue. Sadly, I had to give it up after I could no longer afford to pay the mortgage.

CHAPTER FIFTEEN

Carly and Frank: Doodle Dilemmas

Carly is a middle-aged brown Labradoodle who barks if she sees anything move: squirrel, dog, bird, rabbit, person, leaf.... No matter how many times she is told NO, scolded, or punished with a time-out in her crate, she is unable to desist. And she has a big bark that scares people.

Even though Carly is usually loving and sweet-natured, she has a split personality. If she encounters another dog, she turns from a mild-mannered Dr. Jekyll dog into a sinister Mr. Hyde dog. She lunges, growls, and barks with murderous intent—at least that's how people who don't know her interpret her behavior. They stop or back away. If their dog is small enough, they pick it up to save it from the terrible doodle. I once saw a man yank his Yorkshire Terrier, attached to its collar and leash, up into his arms. I worried about the little dog's neck.

When Carly is with Frank, they are twice as intimidating and nearly impossible to control. Frank is an enormous, blonde, three-year-old Labradoodle. He's the largest doodle I've ever seen. His size is intimidating, although he doesn't look fierce at all—he looks like a big, sweet goofus. But he has a loud, scary voice. Together, Carly and Frank are a formidable pair.

Despite their barking, I love these crazy doodles, and they love me. I've known them since they were puppies. When I arrive at their house, they go giddy with joy. They follow me from room to room. They lean against my legs and sit on my feet. I know they miss their people, but they seem really happy to be with me—maybe because I take them for lots of walks. They love to go for walks. They *need* to go for walks to burn off some of their boundless, bounding, barky energy.

My friend Lynne and her husband live with their German Shepherd on twenty acres a few miles from Bozeman. Lynne's sister Shan lives nearby with her Labradoodle, Grace. Sometimes I take Carly and Frank out there and we all walk in the fields. Twenty acres is a lot of space for a pack of dogs to romp. But the last time I took both doodles, they got too rambunctious with their chasing game. As they ran in circles, mock fighting each other, they slammed into Shan and knocked her face-first into the furrowed stubble of an alfalfa field. Now Carly has to stay home alone while Frank and I go walking with our friends.

When Frank was a puppy, before he learned bad habits from Carly, I used to take them both to Burke Park. We'd walk on the main trail that runs for about a mile along the crest of the hill just east of downtown Bozeman. I kept Carly on a leash and let young Frank romp around and play with other dogs. He always came back when I called him. He never barked or growled at other dogs. But then one day, when he was about eighteen months old, he started acting like Carly. Before I could get them under control, several people had screamed at me to GET THOSE DOGS OUT OF HERE! I'm sure they were terrified. We never again went to Burke Park to walk and play. I needed a new exercise strategy.

■ ■ ■

I decide to take Carly and Frank for separate walks, on a trail near their house. As an added precaution, I restrict our outings to the hours before 6:30 a.m. and after 8 p.m. I figure that's when we're less likely to encounter other dogs.

At 5:30 a.m. I put harnesses on both dogs. I tell Carly to stay, assuring her that it will be her turn next. It's heartbreaking to see her sad eyes as she watches me put the leash on Frank and open the front door to leave with him. As we walk away, I look back and see her gazing mournfully at us through the window.

Frank leaps and dances for joy as we approach the trailhead. I wish I could unclip his leash and let him run. But, even though it's early, I can't be sure no other dogs will be out. And a deer could bolt from its overnight grass bed at any moment, which would be an irresistible pursuit opportunity. We walk along the gravel path for more than a mile. I admire the spectacular colors splashed across the eastern sky while

Frank sniffs every plant. When I get impatient with his sniffing, I remember what the author Ted Kerasote told me during our radio interview about his book, *Merle's Door: Lessons from a Freethinking Dog*. He said that sniffing the neighborhood is to a dog what reading a newspaper is to a person. Using that analogy, I imagine Frank reading with his nose, learning the who, what, when, where, and why of other critters and people who've been here recently.

Science.org offers this fact: Dog noses are up to one hundred million times more sensitive than ours. And a new study reveals that dogs can sense weak thermal radiation—the body heat of mammalian prey—which explains why a blind or deaf dog can still hunt. Cowabunga!

Frank's nose collects important information about the territory he walks through. Yes, he's a pet. But the ancient traits and behaviors of his Poodle and Labrador Retriever instincts still run his body. Labradors and Poodles are both very intelligent. They get bored easily, so mental stimulation (such as reading the canine edition of the local newspaper) is as important for them as physical exercise. A bored doodle becomes a bad doodle, which must be the answer to the question of *why* I'm so determined to find a way to let them run around. I prefer to avoid the mayhem created by bored dogs. Well, that and I also like the challenge of solving a problem. If I encounter obstacles, I look for solutions. And so, we walk at 5:30 a.m.

We make it around the entire trail loop without encountering another dog, which is a relief. When we get back to the house and turn into the driveway, I can see that Carly is still sitting where

I left her. Her nose is literally pressed against the windowpane next to the front door. After I get Frank inside and attach the leash to Carly's harness, I tell him it's her turn to walk. But that is *not* okay with Frank. I can hear him barking all the way to the end of the street. Carly is happy, though. She pees and poops and poses for a photo that shows her long shadow in the light of early morning. She sniffs but doesn't spend as much time at that as Frank does. Not a big reader, apparently.

We are almost back to the house when I see a woman approaching us with a Golden Retriever at her side. We're walking on a short cul-de-sac. There are no sidewalks here, so we're all in the street. The dog beside the woman is not on a leash. Carly emits a low growl.

I stop and say, "No, Carly. Sit." She sits but continues to growl. The woman and the dog are closer now. I wrap the leash around my hips and lean back to keep it taut. "Stay," I say quietly, trying to soothe her anxiety about the other dog. I've wondered if Carly's and Frank's behavior is provoked by anxiety. It's the only reasonable explanation I can think of since they are not mean dogs. "It's okay," I tell her. "Stay. Good girl. Good dog. Everything's okay." She continues to sit, even though she quivers and growls softly. But then the dog crosses some line visible only to Carly.

She leaps forward, barking ferociously.

I lean back against the leash. The woman stops and tells her dog to sit, which it does, immediately. Even though it's not on a leash, it doesn't move a muscle. Carly continues to bark and lunge. It takes all my upper body strength and weight against the leash to keep her from pulling away from me. The woman looks at me with an expression of superiority. Or maybe my imagination paints that expression on her face because I feel so inferior, like an awful, negligent person who would allow a dog to behave so badly. Her dog still hasn't moved.

"This is not my dog," I say, trying to save some face. Why do I say this? I'm not sure. I don't know this woman and her opinion of me shouldn't matter. But still, I continue with, "I'm just taking care of her for a few days." The woman nods and motions for me to continue past her and her silent, obedient dog.

I keep the leash wrapped around my hips and stagger-walk ahead, leaning away from Carly as she lunges sideways, trying to get to the Golden, barking like she wants to kill it.

"She's really a sweet dog," I say to the woman as we pass. Yeah, right, I imagine her thinking as she tells her leash-less dog to "heel" and walks on toward the trailhead.

When we turn onto the street where Carly and Frank live, I can hear Frank barking. He's likely been barking the entire time we were gone. The neighbors are probably pissed. But, right now, I don't really care. It's only 6:15 a.m., and I'm already exhausted. And frustrated.

■ ■ ■

Carly and I arrive at a small, low building that looks fairly new. It's located in a census-designated area called Four Corners, a rapidly growing collection of businesses, storage facilities, warehouses, and subdivisions about eight miles west of downtown Bozeman. We're here for an appointment with a dog trainer I found online. The website offered a free thirty-minute consultation.

A sign on the door tells me to be sure my dog is on a leash before coming inside. We enter through a glass door that leads into a small waiting area lined by wooden benches. There's no one else here. I sit on a bench and tell Carly to sit beside me, which she does—eventually, after investigating some of the fascinating doggy scents in this room.

The door at the back of the room opens and a man enters. He's athletic, fit, probably in his late thirties. His manner is professional. He greets me warmly and bends to pet Carly as she pulls against the leash.

"What are you hoping to get from this session?" he asks me, scratching behind Carly's ears. She sniffs the lower parts of his pant leg with intense concentration.

"I'd like help understanding why this dog growls, barks, and lunges at other dogs like she wants to kill them," I answer. "She's a sweet family dog, but she goes crazy when she sees any other dogs." The man studies Carly for a moment and then looks at me.

"With your permission," he says, "I'd like to see that behavior for myself. Is it okay if I bring in another dog?"

"Sure," I say.

"Okay. I'll be right back." The man turns and opens the door at the back of the room.

Within a few seconds, he returns accompanied by a medium-sized dog that looks like some sort of Border Collie mix. The dog is not on a leash. When Carly sees him, she does her usual thing. The man watches with interest as I do my usual thing: lean against a shortened leash and try to soothe her with words. "No, Carly. It's okay. Look, he's a nice dog. Carly, sit. Sit!"

No matter what I say or do, Carly ignores me and continues to growl, bark, and lunge. The other dog lifts its nose and sniffs in Carly's direction. Otherwise, he doesn't move or react. It's like watching a two-year-old child throw a temper tantrum while a bored parent waits for it to end. When the man has seen enough, he opens the door and tells the other dog to leave the room. He shuts the door and then points at Carly.

"This is a learned pattern of behavior," he says. "A pattern that has never been corrected."

"Okay," I say, eager for a solution. "How can her behavior be corrected?"

The man offers two options for intensive training to break Carly's bad habits and help her learn new skills. One: Bring Carly here to work with a trainer for two hours every day for ten days. Two: Board her here for two weeks, during which time trainers will work with her every day. Both options require "family" training sessions. Carly's people—parents with four young children—would need to learn the new commands and how to be consistent with enforcing those commands. Frank would also have to be trained so he wouldn't continue behaving badly and encourage Carly to return to her old habits. None of this sounds remotely possible for this busy family. But I ask anyway, curious.

"How much do each of these options cost." He gives me a range between $1,200 and $1,500 dollars for the ten-day training session. Per dog. The price tag for the boarding option is, of course, many thousands of dollars higher. Per dog.

Now I know why there are so many badly behaved dogs in the world. I thank the man for his time and pull Carly toward the parking lot. "These are not my dogs," I explain to him. "But I'll pass your name and information on to her people."

Although this solution isn't a good fit for this family, I'm still curious to find out if there's any way I can help. As I said, I love these doodles.

YouTube offers me a gazillion dog training videos. Online sellers offer thousands of dog training books. Dog trainers post advice on social media platforms and blogs. All of them stress the importance of consistency. When you give a dog a command, you must follow through and make sure the dog does what you've told it to do, even if you change your mind. After hours of reading, watching, and listening, I discard the idea that I can add a training component to my pet sitting jobs. Sure, I can train dogs when I'm with them, but all that training will become useless once their people return. Okay then, I decide, once again. I will deal with whatever situation I'm hired for. I don't need to fix any dogs. They are all just fine the way they are, bad habits and all.

And anyway, I wonder how long I'll be able to do this. I'm not a young person. Even though I've done my best to stay healthy and strong, my body's natural loss of muscle mass and agility during the past five years is noticeable. Maybe wrestling with dogs on leashes is the cause of my shoulder pain. Lack of sleep is also an issue.

The calendar on my phone shows that I've slept in my own bed only six of the last thirty nights. Lately, I've resorted to swallowing Ambien and over-the-counter sleep aids, which help me get to sleep, but they have side effects: brain fog and lethargy. I ask myself, almost every day, why I continue to do work that damages my body and brain.

Oh, right. Money.

CHAPTER SIXTEEN

Poop

In 1987, Greg Keeler—a Montana State University-Bozeman English professor, poet, singer-songwriter—wrote and recorded a song titled "No Dog Bathroom" that told the story of a feud between neighbors. In the final verse of the song, the narrator fills a paper bag with a pile of poop that a neighbor's dog deposited on his lawn, puts it on the offender's front porch, and sets it on fire. The song is darkly humorous while pointing out a local sanitation problem.

In the late eighties, dog poop bag dispensers and collection containers were not a thing in Bozeman. I didn't have a dog then, but I saw, and tried not to step on, lots of dog poop when I walked outside—on Peet's Hill, on the Gallagator Trail, and along city sidewalks. Today, plastic bag dispensers are fastened to posts at the beginning of every hiking trail and neighborhood pathway, along with trash containers to dispose

144

of full bags. I greatly appreciate those additions to our urban landscape, and the workers who empty those stinky containers.

I carry poop bags in my backpack or purse and the glove-box of my vehicle. Even when I'm off duty, I find them in the pockets of my jackets and stashed in drawers. Picking up poo is the least appealing part of my critter sitter gigs but it must be done, so I'm always prepared.

Since Keeler released his song, the population of Bozeman has tripled. There is no reliable data for the number of dogs that live here now, but city statistics (based on the number of licenses issued) estimate around twenty-five thousand. Not all the dogs are licensed, though, which makes them difficult to count. Bozeman has a two-dog limit per household. If a resident has more than two dogs, they must buy a "kennel" license from the city. Imagine that paperwork. All cats and chickens are supposed to be licensed, too. I'm sure they are not.

The extra dogs that suddenly appeared in Bozeman during the pandemic population surge created problems: overcrowding on trails and in dog parks, an increase in dog fights and injuries requiring a trip to the vet, and piles of poop left in public places by thoughtless people.

In April of 2023, Gallatin Watershed Council volunteers picked up three hundred and seventy-five gallons of poop along eight of Bozeman's popular walking trails. Thank you, volunteers! That's *three hundred and seventy-five gallons of dog poop* that won't contaminate our water with chemical nutrients from pet food, medications, pathogens, and bacteria, such as E. coli. Canine feces aren't the only poopy pollution in Western Montana's water, however.

Sewage from the homes of the rich and famous—members of the ritzy Yellowstone Club near Big Sky, Montana—ends up in the Gallatin River. Not as a direct discharge, of course, because that's illegal. Instead, it enters the river as run-off from the Yellowstone Club's over-irrigated golf course, which is watered with treated sewage. They must get rid of it somehow and this was their solution: spray it onto the greens and fairways.

Finding ways to get rid of waste from the Yellowstone Club has been a problem since the beginning of its development. In 1993, the Montana Department of Health and Human Services (now the Department of Environmental Quality) placed a moratorium on construction in the Big Sky area because the sewage holding ponds leaked. The watersheds in the area are listed as "impaired streams," but that hasn't stopped developers and realtors from pushing their projects. Many of them blast through environmental obstacles by sitting on advisory boards and holding public office.

Over the years, bizarre solutions to the sewage problems have been proposed. The latest, and (to me) most bizarre, is the idea to make snow from treated sewage and blow it onto Eglise Mountain. What?! Where do they think that prescription-drug-laced snow will end up if not in a river? According to numerous sources, the sewage treatment technology to remove all traces of prescription drugs has not yet been invented. Think fish, elk, birds, and grizzly bears ingesting anti-depressants, hormones, antibiotics, and high blood pressure meds with their river water. At least one lawsuit has been filed.

Organizations such as Cottonwood Environmental Law Center, and many others, continue to work on legal strategies aimed at keeping Montana's rivers clean—a huge challenge when BIG money is at stake. But what if a common citizen objects to environmental pollution and doesn't have the money or the desire to start a nonprofit organization or initiate a lawsuit?

Well then, that person might, as Greg Keeler did, use art as a weapon and write a bluesy song with some red-hot lyrics:

...I jumped off of my porch and screamed, Not on my lawn!
This is No Dog Bathroom, No Dog Bathroom...
You wanna empty that dog, you better find some other place...
Well the next time your dog's hunching over my lawn
I'm gonna gather up his goodies and as soon as he's gone
I'll put 'em in a paper bag and follow him home
I'll sneak up on your porch and when I'm sure I'm alone
I'll set that bag on fire and ring your doorbell
And when you stomp it out I'll be laughin' like hell...

CHAPTER SEVENTEEN

Zola and Fendi

Zola must be psychic. Somehow, he knows I'm about to leave the house. But how? I made sure he was out in the back yard with Fendi before I carried my stuff out to the garage. The sliding glass door was shut. There's no way he could have seen my getting-ready-to-leave activities. And yet, even though I've tried every trick I can think of to get him to come back inside the house, he's not falling for any of them. I check the time. Yikes! I have a thirty-minute drive to get to an appointment, which starts in forty-five minutes.

"Hey, Zola," I call to him in my most enticing voice, "come on, boy! Let's get some treats!" He stands in the middle of the lawn holding a blue and white stuffed octopus in his mouth. For him, playtime isn't over. He isn't ready to come into the boring house. How does he know I'm about to leave? He has always come when I've called him inside.

Zola is the most enormous German Shepherd I've ever seen. And I have seen *a lot* of German Shepherd dogs. He's named after the French novelist Émile Zola. It takes me a while to get used to Zola as a name for a male dog. I keep wanting to call him a her. Zola's canine housemate is a small, chubby dog with stiff black and white hair. Fendi's person told me she's named after a high-end handbag. I had never heard of anything called a Fendi, but Google tells me it's an "Italian luxury fashion house producing fur, ready-to-wear, leather goods, shoes, fragrances, eyewear, timepieces, and accessories."

At fendi.com I discover that people will pay from $1,500 to $6,000, and beyond, for the privilege of owning a Fendi purse. A *purse*! This amazes and alarms me. The website shows a small, black purse with a price tag of $6,280. OMG. It's not decorated with diamonds or precious jewels or metal. It looks like it's made of woven leather. I understand the value of original designs, but, still, the prices seem excessive. Maybe the clasp is made of solid gold?

The name of this dog must be an inside joke because these people live in a quiet middle-class suburb north of Belgrade. I feel much more comfortable in this modest split-level suburban house than in any of the other houses I've stayed in during the past few months, most of which were ginormous.

Fendi is an obedient and reasonable dog, highly motivated by treats, as proven by her ample girth. Thirty minutes ago, when I called Fendi and Zola into the house, she came right in, crunched through her treat, and then settled into a nap on the back of the couch. But no treat or trickery has persuaded

Zola to come inside. I'm getting desperate. I need to get on the road soon if I'm going to get to my appointment on time.

A few minutes ago, Zola came up the stairs and stood on the deck just outside the open sliding glass door to the kitchen. He listened to me, ears erect, head cocked to one side, while I asked, invited, and finally commanded him to come inside. But he wouldn't walk through the door. This is not a dog I can physically wrestle into the house. He looks like he weighs over a hundred pounds. He is solid muscle. When I tried to move him forward with one hand on his collar and one hand pushing on his hind end, he wouldn't budge. It felt like trying to push a concrete lawn ornament through the door.

Now I yell, "Zola COME!" in my best authoritative voice. He ignores me, drops the toy octopus, and starts sniffing at some fascinating, invisible thing in the grass. "Zola," I call from the top of the stairway that descends from the deck into the yard. "Please come in. Good boy!" He continues to ignore me. I hurry down the stairs and walk across the grass, intending to clip a leash to his collar. He acts like we're playing a game of keep-away, bouncing around me in circles while I plead with him to hold still.

I can't leave Zola in the yard. My instructions are to lock both dogs inside the house when I'm away. Anyway, I'll worry if I leave him outside until I return. I also noticed a webcam mounted under the deck. The people who live here might be watching me right now. Just in case they *are* watching, I quit the keep-away game and pick up the octopus. "Hey, look!" I say, waggling it at Zola. "Go get it!" I throw the octopus toward the steps. Zola isn't fooled. He saunters off toward the back of the yard.

I have to to leave now! What am I going to do? I'm out of ideas. But wait. Am I really out of ideas? Think, think, think… what does he want? What does Zola want? Oh, right!

Inside the house, there's a black metal gate at the top of the steep, narrow stairway that leads down to the front door of this split-level house. That gate, I was told, is supposed to be closed at all times. It's there to keep the dogs from knocking people over on the steep, narrow stairway. They like to rush down the stairs to greet everyone. Zola and Fendi are very enthusiastic about visitors.

Whenever I open that gate, Zola comes running. He loves to go down the stairs. Downstairs is where the garage is, the place where car rides to hiking trails originate. Downstairs is where the home office is, a place where he gets to hang out while his guy works.

The gate to downstairs has a metal latch on it. Bingo! I just need that sound. I find a ball, walk up the stairs, and toss the ball from the deck onto the grass below. Zola bounds across the lawn, grabs it in his mouth, and runs back up the stairs.

"Ready to come in?" I ask him, hopefully. He doesn't move toward me or drop the ball for me to throw again. "No? Okay." He watches me go inside. I slide the glass door nearly shut, leaving an opening just wide enough for Zola to fit through. I walk over to the gate at the top of the stairs and lift the small metal bar that fits into the metal catch piece that locks the gate. I drop the bar, making as much noise as possible. When he hears the clang, Zola rushes through the door and across the kitchen, aiming for the gate. I sprint past him and slide the patio door closed. Voila!

Back at the gate, I lean down to pet Zola. "Good boy!" I say softly into one of his ears while rubbing his other ear just the way he likes it. "Very good boy. I'm so sorry you have to stay inside. Sorry I tricked you. "But," I add in a high, cheerful voice, "I'll be back soon. You stay with Fendi and be a good boy." Zola's eyes remain fixed on the gate. His body leans toward it, tensed and ready. "No," I tell him. "You stay. Stay!"

When I lift the latch, Zola tries to push past me, nearly knocking me down the stairs. I throw my knee into his chest and ease through the gate far enough to click it shut behind me.

"Sorry Zola," I say, again as I lose my balance and fall against the wall at the top of the stairway. When I'm upright again I reach over the gate to give Zola a final ear scratch. He looks pathetic. "Go lie down on your bed," I say, pointing. He continues to admonish me with his big, glistening brown eyes. "Okay, then. See you later." I start down the stairs. "Bye Fendi." Fendi lifts her head for one second and then drops back into her nap.

When I turn the corner on the landing, ready to walk down the next set of stairs and out to the garage, I see that Zola is still waiting in front of the gate, ever hopeful.

■ ■ ■

Most people tell me to "eat anything you find in the refrigerator or cupboards." And I take them at their word. After greeting the pets and setting my laptop bag on the dining room table, one of the first things I do is to look inside the fridge and pantry. Even though I recognize this behavior as a habit formed long ago, during my teenage babysitting years, it's a challenge to stop myself.

As a growing tween and teen, I was constantly hungry. Yes, my parents fed me, but never enough. They were on a tight budget. I took babysitting jobs mostly so I could eat other people's food. The people I babysat for always told me to help myself to whatever I could find in the kitchen. At five-feet-eleven-inches tall and one-hundred-ten pounds, I'm sure I looked hungry. At the very least, too skinny. What a difference other people's kitchens were from my house where my housewife mother guarded the food—she always seemed to be in the kitchen—and my frugal father, who did all the grocery shopping, rationed the rations.

I did not *want* to babysit. I had six younger siblings at home, for Pete's sake. Babysitter was my middle name. But I did want money, and I did want access to more food.

During these past few months of near-constant critter sitting, I've gained fifteen pounds. Not because of how *much* I've eaten but because of *what* I've eaten. In my condo, there are no chips, crackers, cookies, cold cereal, chocolate chips (why does all the good stuff begin with the letter "C"), or raisins in my cupboards. Not even a loaf of bread. Buttered toast is my nemesis. There's no ice cream in my freezer. No cheeses, flavored yogurts, juice, milk, or pudding in the refrigerator. I have no willpower to resist any of that stuff. I will eat any of those foods before one piece of a vegetable goes into my mouth. In my twenties, I often went several days without eating a single vegetable. Not because I didn't like them but because they were too much trouble to prepare (in the days before we could buy bags of salad and pre-cut produce in grocery stores). I had things to do! And my mouth yearns for the sensations of crunchy, sweet, salty, and creamy.

In my thirties—after several cycles of gaining and losing many extra pounds—I stopped buying problem foods, mostly. So, I don't keep any of the aforementioned in my own kitchen. But apparently, most other people don't have food addiction issues. They can put whatever they want into their refrigerators and cupboards without hearing it constantly call out to them: Eat me, eat me, EAT ME!

Zola's and Fendi's people are active young professionals. One look inside their pantry, and I know I'm in trouble. The shelves are packed with Costco-size containers of M&Ms, Cheez-its, cookies, trail mix, several types of cold cereal, and a loaf of bread. Inside the fridge is a nearly full carton of milk to pour on the cold cereals. Cold cereal is my weakest food weakness. When floating in milk, it is simultaneously crunchy, sweet, salty, and creamy. There's also a pan of left-over lasagna, five different kinds of white and yellow cheeses, and a brick of cream cheese. Cheese is another of my worst weaknesses. On the bottom shelf of the fridge are three cartons of sugary, fruit-flavored yogurt. The freezer contains several Zip-loc bags full of bagels, cut in half and ready for the toaster, and a plastic container filled with chocolate-chip cookies.

In a large room on the lower level of the house, I discover what looks like the wine section of a small grocery store covering most of one wall. The downstairs fridge is full of specialty beers, cans of sparkling water and sodas, and ingredients for mixed drinks. Upstairs, there's a well-stocked liquor cabinet in the kitchen. They also told me to "help yourself" to the wine, beer, and liquor. They had too much, they said, left over from their recent wedding. It's a good thing I don't have the physical ability to tolerate much alcohol.

I stand in the kitchen stunned by the quantity and proximity of all this tasty food I rarely allow myself to eat. Zola, who has followed me down the stairs and back up again during my self-guided tour of the house, drops the stuffed giraffe he's been carrying in his mouth onto my foot.

"Thanks for the distraction, big boy," I say to him. Eating food I don't need can wait for a few minutes. I reach down to pat his head and grab the toy. "It's time for some fetch!"

Fendi jumps down from her perch on the back of the couch and follows us to the sliding glass door that opens onto the deck. Fendi hops, one at a time, down the stairs on her short, little legs. She quickly pees and walks under the nearest bush to sniff at its roots.

The house sits on a half-acre lot, so the yard is big. This place is part of a subdivision built on prime farmland during the 1970s. Very few people were concerned about the loss of farmland or urban sprawl in the Gallatin Valley back then. At the time, Montana was a vast state where less than seven-hundred-thousand people shared more than ninety-four million acres. A handful of streets run through this neighborhood, which includes a large, grassy park with the usual playground equipment: swings, teeter totter, merry-go-round, slide, and hanging bars. It's a family-oriented island of suburbia loosely surrounded by agriculture, airport acreage, newer subdivisions, and a few industrial enterprises.

The chain link fence around this property is lined with trees and bushes. It looks like an experienced gardener once tended abundant flowerbeds filled with perennials, but now it's all gone wild. While Fendi inspects roots and leaves, Zola prances beside me on the deck, waiting for me to throw his toy.

"Okay. Go get it!" I say, tossing the stuffed giraffe as far out into the yard as I can. Zola has to run down the steep stairs and across the lawn to retrieve it. That'll take him a while, I think, stepping back into the kitchen without closing the door. But he is fast. I've barely opened the refrigerator door when he appears beside me, giraffe in mouth.

My next throw launches the giraffe up into an Aspen tree. It lands between two branches and sticks there, too high up for me to reach with a broom handle or any other tool I find in the garage and laundry room. But Zola doesn't miss a beat. When he can't find the giraffe anywhere on the ground, he roots around in the bushes until he finds a hedgehog. He runs up the stairs, drops it on the deck, and trots through the open door and into the house. Seconds later he's back at my side with a ball. No worries, he seems to say. We have lots of toys.

I throw toys and balls into the backyard for what feels like hours. Zola runs up and down the steep stairway—from the deck to the yard and back up—an uncountable number of times and never looks tired, not for one second. Fendi reappears. She walks inside the house and flops onto Zola's bed, which is enormous. She looks like a black and white leaf floating on a gray pond, but she rules the space like an imperious Queen. I'm beginning to think her name is a good match for her personality.

That night, as I lie in the guest room bed—a *really* comfy bed, thankfully—I can't get to sleep. My right arm aches from throwing toys and balls for Zola. If he had his way, we'd never stop. I kept telling him "No" and he kept nudging my leg and dropping a toy or a ball at my feet, interrupting my meal of lasagna and peanut M&Ms. I wonder if his people let him bully them into endless playtime, or if he's testing my boundaries. Most likely the latter, and I've failed the test. But even though I know he's probably manipulating me, I can't resist his charm, large brown eyes, and expressive face. I am such a pushover. Yes, I am. And a pleaser.

■ ■ ■

The next day, as I'm looking for plastic poo bags, I spot a ball-thrower on a shelf in the garage. Eureka! This device makes playtime much easier. Gripping the long orange plastic handle, I use both arms to fling the ball across the big yard. I'm hoping Zola will lose it in the bushes for a while, but he doesn't. His über-sensitive German Shepherd nose finds it every time and he hurries back to me, eager for the next toss.

Even after chasing balls all day, Zola continues his campaign for more playtime that evening while I sit on the couch watching *The Mandalorian* on DisneyPlus. Like most houses where dogs live, this house includes a large basket filled with toys: stuffed animals, oddly shaped plastic things that squeak, tennis balls, and rubber bones. Each time I ignore a toy Zola drops on the cushion next to me, he trots off to get another one. Soon, there's a mob of slobber-soaked objects piled next to my legs. Yuck. Meanwhile, Fendi is curled up on top of the couch cushion behind my head, snoring softly. She's so easy, it's almost like I'm only taking care of one dog.

I need to set some boundaries with Zola. My right shoulder really hurts. I've been throwing balls, sticks, and toys for months now, and my schedule is packed with critter sitting for the next three months. Lots of dogs means lots of ball throwing. A massage therapist I found online gave me some relief. After three therapeutic treatments, my shoulder felt a lot better. I really need a weekly massage, but my insurance won't pay for it. I make a note in the calendar app on my phone to contact my primary care physician for a referral to a physical therapist, which insurance *will* pay for. In the meantime, I swallow ibuprofen and vow to get better at left-handed ball throwing.

■ ■ ■

The next morning, right after breakfast, Zola begins his relentless requests for play time. A cup of green tea is cooling next to my laptop. I have a client deadline. I do not want to throw balls or toys. But Zola looks mortally wounded when I tell him no. His brown eyes glisten and plead.

"Don't look at me like that!" I say loudly. Fendi's head pops up. She jumps off the couch and hurries over to see what's happening. Now she's looking at me, too. Crikey. I can't deal with sad-dog eyes. "Okay. You guys win." I take a sip of tea, grab the ball flinger, and open the sliding glass door to the deck.

It's a late-September morning, sunny, and almost warm enough. The cloudless sky is brilliant and blue and clear. A whisper of wind carries a hint of chill and wood smoke. I pull on a sweater and step out onto the deck, leaving the door open. I have a plan. Fendi trots past me and down the stairs. She pees and begins her long, habitual investigation of each bit of vegetative debris in the yard. I can hear crackling as she steps on dried leaves and twigs under the first lilac bush.

Zola eyes are fixed on me. He pants and prances in anticipation. His big tongue drips and pulses. "Okay boy," I say, looking him in the eye. "You ready?" Of course he's ready! He's always ready.

Wielding the flinger with my left arm, I lob a few practice balls into the yard. Each time I throw, Zola quickly descends the steep stairway, runs out across the lawn, and then back up the steps. His toenails make a clickity sound on the painted wood. I can feel the deck vibrate as his considerable weight hits each step. He is fast. But maybe I can slow him down. After a few short throws, I use both arms and aim for the back of the yard, at a stretch of fence flanked by a thick tangle of bushes. I fling the ball as hard and fast as I can. It lands inside a bush at the far end of the yard. I hurry back inside the kitchen and set the flinger on the countertop next to the door.

I jump onto the stool in front of my laptop and take a quick sip of tea. I glance through the list of new email messages, star the ones that need an immediate response, open the first message, and begin to type. I hear clickity-clickity on the deck and then Zola appears in the doorway. He drops the ball and waits. I take another sip of tea, stand, and mash the flinger onto the ball. Fling, sit, sip, type, stand. Repeat.

Each throw gives me only a couple of minutes to focus on my work, but it's valuable time. A few years ago, I discovered how productive I could be in two-minute segments—one-handed—when I began using an electric toothbrush. While the toothbrush does its work, I can make the bed, toss a load of laundry into the washing machine, transfer clothes to the dryer, clean the bathroom sink or mirror, fill the portable humidifier with water, or Swiffer a few pieces of furniture—any of the tasks I've done so many thousands of times that my brain can navigate them without much participation from me. I'm aware of what experts say about multi-tasking, but the experts didn't know Mrs. Benson.

Mrs. Benson was one of my piano teachers. She taught me to play scales with both hands in two against three rhythms. It wasn't easy. As I struggled, she told me to use my imagination to divide my brain in half, and then to imagine each half of my brain connected to one of my hands: the left side connected to my left hand and the right side connected to my right hand. It worked. Eventually, that trick allowed me to play two notes of the scale with my left hand while simultaneously playing three notes with my right hand. Mrs. Benson's visualization technique helped me then, and it still does.

If anyone had told my younger self that practicing scales on the piano would someday help me with housework or throwing balls for a dog, there's no way I would have believed it. But it's true. It's also true that, although my condo is clean and tidy, I don't like cleaning or the work of keeping things tidy. To me, housework—like putting on makeup or chewing food—is a repetitive, never-ending task that uses time I could spend on something much more fun. I'd rather enjoy activities with family and friends, work on creative projects, hike, bike, play music. Almost anything else seems like a better use of my time than housework, make-up, and chewing. Since housework and chewing are necessary, I do them. But spend my time in front of a make-up mirror? *Never.* Although I truly admire women who apply make-up skillfully. They look great! If only I cared that much about how my face looks to other people. But I don't. What I do care about is experiences. And right now, I want to experience throwing a ball for Zola while editing a podcast.

This experiment might seem ridiculous to someone else (undoubtedly), but I enjoy a challenge. Breaking focus on a work project every two minutes is difficult, but this is research. Let's see what happens.

■ ■ ■

Zola stands on the deck with a ball in his mouth, looking at me through the open kitchen door. He drops the ball. It rolls slowly toward the edge of the deck. Quickly, he snatches it back and drops it in front of the door again. I ignore him, but I can feel his eyes on me. These two-minute work breaks have been somewhat successful during the past hour. I'm getting stuff done. Unfortunately, for Zola, my response time hasn't been immediate. With podcast editing, I need to find a break point and mark it before I turn my attention back to ball flinging. Zola is patient, though.

He waits, stares at me, tongue dripping, panting, hoping I'll get back into the game. Somehow, the back half of his body is turned toward the stairs, ready for action, while his head and shoulders face me. By now, the morning sun has heated the deck and warmed the kitchen. After all that stair running and sprinting across the yard, Zola must be hot in his thick fur coat. But he is not ready to quit. I don't think he will ever quit. Until bedtime, that is, which is thirteen hours from now.

I delete a lip smack and one more "uhm" from the interview I'm editing and glance over at Zola. The expression on his face is simultaneously eager and serene. Weird.

"I'll be with you in just a minute," I tell him. "Almost done. Thanks for waiting."

An old song begins to play in my mind: "If it takes forever, I will wait for you. For a thousand summers I will wait for you... " The song is from a 1964 French musical, but I must know it from hearing the English version recorded by Connie Francis, a popular singer in the late 1960s. A French song for a German Shepherd dog named after a French novelist. Perfect.

I click "save," stand up, and grab the ball. As I launch it into the bushes at the back of the yard, I sing to Zola:

In your heart believe,
What in my heart I know.
That forevermore I will wait for you.

CHAPTER EIGHTEEN

The Critter Sitter Job Description

I'm not sure a job description for the position of critter sitter could ever be all-inclusive. It doesn't seem possible to list every skill and bit of knowledge a person might need when dealing with people and their pets, as well as the rules and problems associated with each unique house and property. But here are the highlights:

1. Education. A university degree in psychology or social work will be helpful. At the very least, you should be smart and resourceful, able to deal with unexpected situations and navigate the quirky behavior of people and animals.

2. Experience. Life experience is your most important resource as a critter sitter. The longer you've been alive, the more problems you've solved. You'd be surprised

how often a seemingly insignificant experience from your past can solve a present-day dilemma. You should have a well-honed ability to learn from the mistakes you weren't smart enough to avoid. Good housekeeping skills are essential, too—especially experience with carpet cleaning products and knowledge of how to use them without causing permanent damage or discoloration to handmade wool and cotton rugs. You should know how to properly launder various household items and fabrics, especially cashmere and silk. Knowledge about the proper care of cast iron cookware, cooktop surfaces, concrete countertops, and natural woods will also come in handy.

3. Knowledge. You'll need to understand various types of dog breeds—their propensities, typical behaviors, and emotional needs. Each kind of dog has been bred, sometimes for centuries, to emphasize specific qualities. It's helpful to know what to expect. If you're unfamiliar with a particular breed, do some online research. Cats are…cats. They are less likely to conform categorizations.

4. High tolerance for yuck. Part of the job is to clean up vomit, pee, soupy feces, and gooey hairballs. And to pick up warm, steaming piles of poop with a plastic bag or pooper scooper. You should be able to wield a shovel and deftly slide sticky clumps of dog poop into a five-gallon bucket or other type of container. Depending on the length of your stay, you'll also need

to transfer rotting shit to a trash container before the weekly pickup. Failure to do so will create a stinky situation your clients will not appreciate when they return.

5. Curiosity. It's very important to find out where the pet supplies are before you're on the job: food, poo bags, leashes, treats, toys, medications, etcetera. Some people will forget to tell you important and obvious information because it's all automatic to them. (I once had to text a person to ask where the dog's food was after I searched all the obvious places. It was, *duh*, under the sink in the master bathroom.) Information about the type of animal you're caring for is helpful, too. Do some online research if the breed is new to you. Ask the people to explain how their house's heating and cooling systems function. And the appliances. And the entertainment system. Find out if housekeepers or yard maintenance or other service people are expected to arrive on the property during your stay. You want to avoid calling the police when you see a guy in the yard who's only there to blow out the sprinkler system.

6. Stamina. Unless you are caring for a very elderly animal, expect to throw balls, walk or hike, chase after, and repeatedly open doors for pets. Some pets will require lots of brushing, soothing, and petting. Expect sleep disruption, both from sleeping in an unfamiliar bed in an unfamiliar environment and from pets who hog the bed, purr on your pillow, or walk across you

during the night. No matter what time you go to bed, expect to be awakened at dawn.

7. Adaptability. This is not a job for an inflexible or intolerant person.

8. Social skills. Be prepared to respond with compassion, kindness, and professionalism to any situation that arises, no matter how inconvenient or bizarre. Social media, Google reviews, and references are real. Your name is associated with a business service and is directly linked to future income and your professional reputation. Even if critter sitting is a temporary gig, you don't want to leave digital evidence for a prospective employer to find.

9. Other duties as assigned. Impossible to identify until they appear. These include medical emergencies, equipment malfunctions, hunger strikes, and behavior that's odd or unfamiliar, even to the pet's people.

10. Luck. A shit ton of luck.

CHAPTER NINETEEN

Jasmine and Krista: It Helps to Know What You're Dealing With

Jasmine whines and rakes her front claws across my black cotton leggings. "Knock it off!" I say, shaking my leg and looking down at her with a stern face. She pauses for about ten seconds and then resumes whining and scratching furiously at my left shin. Jasmine is a small dog. Even though she's standing on her hind legs and stretching her light brown body upward as far as possible, her front paws only reach as far as my knee.

I'm perched on a stool at the kitchen island—a vast slab of granite approximately the size of the entire kitchen in my condo—eating a tuna sandwich while Jasmine repeatedly scrapes her claws against my legs and whines. I'm pretty sure I know what she wants, but I won't hold a dog on my lap while I eat. And I'm not sharing my lunch. Lines must be drawn.

Quite obviously, though, being relegated to the floor isn't what Jasmine is used to. She exudes an attitude of entitlement. The smell of tuna might be a trigger, but I don't believe it's food she's really after. I think she has lap privileges while the people here eat and do whatever else they do while sitting on the high-backed, upholstered stools at this counter. The woman of the house, the person who interviewed me, seemed exceptionally attached to Jasmine. Now, Jasmine is acting like my refusal to pick her up is totally unbelievable.

Meanwhile, Krista, a middle-aged yellow lab, the other dog I'm responsible for, lounges on the thick blue area rug under the dining table. She wants nothing to do with Jasmine's lap-time campaign. Krista reserves her enthusiasm for treats and tennis balls. And sunshine. Every fifteen minutes, or so, she scoots a few inches across the floor, following the light as it traverses the room. The happy lab doesn't seem to care that her people are gone. If someone, anyone, is here to feed her and throw balls, she's happy. I think. Maybe. It's hard to tell since I've never lived with her before.

"Good girl, Krista," I say as I step around Jasmine and carry my empty lunch plate to the sink. "Thanks for being so mellow yellow.' I launch into the song, in my best Donovan voice. "They call me mellow yellow (quite rightly). They call me mellow yellow." Krista lifts her head, looks at me for a second, and then closes her eyes. The things I have to put up with, I imagine her thinking as she returns to her nap.

Jasmine circles my feet anxiously. I reach down and pick her up. "Sorry your people are gone, Jaz. Sorry you're stuck with me." She licks my cheek with her tiny pink tongue. As long as she's not on the floor, she's happy. But back to the floor she goes. I need both hands for kitchen cleanup.

After lunch, I return to the counter, to my laptop and another work session. Jasmine follows and takes up her position at my feet. I also refuse to work with a dog on my lap, even though Jasmine pleaded her case thoroughly this morning. Hello! I don't want bits of pet hair gunking up my keyboard, not to mention the irritation of reaching around a dog, even a small dog, to type and mouse. I've only been in this house for three hours, and it looks like the next five days will be a challenge. It would have been helpful to get more information about this little canine princess before her people left. But she acted much different with me during my interview: friendly, relaxed, and affectionate. Now she's trying to crawl up my leg every moment, acting like a child afraid of monsters in the closet.

There's a home office next to the living room area of this enormous, aptly named, great room. Maybe Jasmine will be happier if I work in there. I remember seeing one of her dog beds next to the desk. I carry my laptop, etcetera, into the office. Jasmine runs after me. She hops around the room in anticipation as I set everything on the desk. As soon as my butt hits the seat of the Herman Miller Aeron chair, she begins to dance on her hind legs, stretching her body toward me, begging me to pick her up. I give her a gentle shove toward the puffy, green plaid circle on the floor.

"Get on your bed," I say. "Time for a nap." But she's not having it. She ducks away from my hand and turns back to paw at my leg. "Oh, for...I give up." I lift her onto my lap. "Alrighty then. Let's get to work." She settles onto my thighs with a contented sigh. I can imagine Jasmine spending long hours in this office while her person responds to email messages and makes phone calls—she and her person comfortable and happy together. But nothing about this workspace is comfortable for me.

The desk and office chair are a good fit for the woman who lives here, because she's seven or eight inches shorter than me, but I can't get comfortable. Also, the lighting is awful. The glare from the south-facing window hurts my eyes, and yet, somehow, it doesn't throw much useable light into the room. There's no lamp on the desk and the fixtures on the ceiling are twenty feet away. I slide my page of editing notes around, searching for the right amount of light, shading my eyes against the glare. I want to work in this room at this desk, for Jasmine's sake. She looks so peaceful and content on my lap. Within a few minutes, however, my shoulders and neck ache from reaching around her. Every time I shift my position, one of my knees slams into the metal rail that attaches the middle drawer to the desk.

Finally, when I can't stand it anymore, I lift Jasmine off my lap and set her on the floor. She blinks in confusion as I gather my stuff and move it all back to the kitchen counter.

■ ■ ■

Jasmine puts up with my refusal to work and eat while holding her on my lap for thirty-six hours. And then, it's game on!

171

First, she pees on the carpet in the master bedroom, which is on the main floor. The yellow spot is positioned just inside the room, nicely centered in the doorway where I can see it when I walk by on my way to the kitchen in the morning. I thought she'd spent the night upstairs, snuggled next to my hip on the bed in the guest room. That's where she was when I went to sleep and woke up. But I guess she went for a nocturnal walkabout, even though her bladder should have been empty. I took both dogs outside just before bedtime and *watched* them both pee. She must have gone downstairs during the night and slurped up half a bowl of water to accomplish this defiant deed.

Second, she poops on the living room carpet—during the day, shortly after we'd all been out the yard for nearly an hour.

Third, she drags one of the woman's sandals out of the shoe cubby in the front hallway, carries it into the living room, chews through a strap, and chomps the decorative button into splinters.

She also barks a lot. When we're inside, she barks at whatever she sees through the floor-to-ceiling windows that are everywhere on the main floor of this house, including the front entryway. When we're out in the yard, she barks at sage hens huddled in the tall grasses next to the golf course. She barks at other dogs, the UPS delivery guy, a bird flying through the sky, kids riding bikes on the street…basically, anything that moves.

Part of my job is to soothe anxiety—for both people and pets. The people are easy. I can soothe them with reassuring text messages and cute photos of their beloved critters. But how can I explain to a pet that its people have just gone away for a few days or weeks, that they'll be back soon? What does the word "soon" mean to a dog? Nada. Jasmine is punishing me because I'm not giving her what she wants. I'm not giving her the focused attention she's used to because I didn't know anything about her expectations or requirements.

When a dog's people are away, I assume nothing feels normal to them—because nothing *is* normal. I do my best to keep to their usual food, play, and sleep schedules, but I'll never meet their expectations. Because I am *not* their person. Even if I pet and cuddle them all day long, their people are still missing. But at least they're in their own house—where everything is familiar—instead of in a strange environment, such as a boarding kennel. Right? That must be what the people think, anyway, or they wouldn't have hired me. Is that true, though?

For Zak the cat and his German Shepherds, home is best because Zak sinks into a state of depression when his dogs are gone. They're a unique trio of pets, though. I wonder if staying home actually helps most dogs cope with the fact that their people are missing. At home, they're constantly reminded that nothing is normal. At a kennel, in a completely different environment, they might be distracted by new dogs to play with and unusual activities. Of course, there's always nighttime, which might bring on fearfulness. Most pets are used to sleeping near their people—if not in the same bed, then at least in the same room. (Jack, the Irish Setter, being an exception.) Every dog is different, though. They each have their own personality and preferences. Some of those preferences are characteristic of the breed—for example, Jasmine, a Cavalier King Charles Spaniel.

This is the first time I've taken care of a Cavalier King Charles Spaniel. Before I came to this house, I'd never even met one. I need information. What I find out online makes sense: "They are very dependent dogs—often too dependent. When they feel abandoned, they become anxious, which they express by chewing destructively and barking." Another site states, "this type of dog is prone to separation anxiety and may engage in destructive behaviors." Geez. What have I gotten myself into?

And then I find this gem: "the Cavalier loves to cuddle and has been described as the perfect lap dog." I didn't know I'd signed up for five days of forced lap time. How different my time here could have been if the people had given me *any* of this information. I'm not sure I'd have taken the job if I'd known I couldn't do my freelance work at their house or eat meals without traumatizing their dog. But wait. Is it up to me to find information about dogs I'm not familiar with before accepting a pet sitting job? Possibly.

However, working on my freelance projects while taking care of other people's pets is part of the deal. Most people like this deal because it means I'll spend more time with their cherished animals. *I* initially liked the deal because it meant I had two income streams. Now I'm not so sure. The math doesn't look good.

At first, these high-paying gigs seemed like a gift from the universe. But when I divide my daily rate of pay by twenty-four hours a day, it comes out to less than four dollars an hour. Factor in fuel and vehicle maintenance, taxes and Social Security payments, the cost of the memory foam mattress topper I had to buy to put on top of a few intolerably uncomfortable beds, reduced productivity due to lack of sleep and anxiety…I'm not sure this is a good deal for me—financially, mentally, or emotionally.

Also, all the time I spend tending to pets in direct ways— ball throwing, walks, feeding, petting, picking up poo, taking cute pet pics, texting with their people before, during, and after the gig, etcetera—is time I'm not using to promote my audio production and writing services. What would happen if I put more effort into that? Hmmm…. .

If only all the dogs were like Krista. She's easy. Mostly. She just wants to chase balls, go for walks, sniff the heck out of everything, have her ears rubbed, and eat. And eat.

Twice a day, Krista waits—poised for action—for Jasmine to walk away from her bowl so she can rush over and gobble up the rest of the food. One of my assigned duties is to make sure Krista *does not* eat Jasmine's food. Jasmine loves to taunt Krista (and torture me) by eating as slowly as possible, looking around the room or walking a few steps away from the dish in between bites. I have to stand far enough away from Jasmine so she'll pay attention to eating (if I sit, she'll come over for lap time), but close enough to be sure Krista doesn't get to the left-over food before I can grab the bowl and set it on the counter. This irritating, twice-daily routine requires patience, precision timing, the ability to stomp down my feelings of exasperation, and fifteen to thirty minutes of my focused attention. That's a lot of time for food dish monitoring.

My commitment to this line of work wiffle waffles with a new level of intensity.

■ ■ ■

Jasmine and Krista wear invisible fence collars, so I don't have to deal with leashes unless we leave the yard. We all go outside many times each day. They both seem happier outside. Jasmine doesn't whine or demand to be picked up. She sniffs around the perimeter of the house, barks at birds and people, and chases after Krista while Krista chases after the tennis balls I throw.

When we're inside, I do my best to reassure both dogs with lots of petting, cuddle time (when I'm not working or eating), and extra treats. At night, we snuggle on the couch and watch *Star Wars* movies and episodes of the old *Gilmore Girls* series. I talk to them constantly. Does that help? Who knows. Every morning, I update them on the countdown: the number of days or hours until their people will be home. I don't think Krista cares, but Jasmine is perpetually unsettled. Poor thing.

■ ■ ■

When I leave this house, my instructions are to put Jasmine and Krista into the huge family room on the second floor and close the door. Jasmine gets to roam around freely inside the room, but I'm supposed to put Krista into the large crate with a cushy blanket on the bottom of it. The first time I'm ready to leave, Krista obeys my request to come up the stairs and get into the crate. The next time, however, she sits at the bottom of the stairs and looks up at me. No amount of coaxing convinces her to move.

"Come on, Krista," I plead from the top of the stairs. "I have to go. Please come up here like the very good girl I know you are." Not only does she not come up the stairs, but she flops down on the floor with a defiant look on her face. The third time I ask, she rolls onto her side and pretends to sleep.

I hurry down the stairs and get behind her. I bend over and slide her body next to the bottom step. She stays limp. I pick up her front paws and place them on the first step. Then I hoist her rear end off the floor. It seems like a futile thing to do because I know I can't lift this seventy-pound dog up even one step, much less carry her to the second floor. But my determination must be apparent because Krista heaves a heavy sigh, stands, and walks, as slowly as possible, up the stairs and into her crate.

Score one for the critter sitter!

■ ■ ■

The weather turns cold the day before the people are scheduled to return. I can't figure out how to heat this behemoth of a house. No matter how high I set the digital thermostat it doesn't get warmer in any of the rooms. There's a "settings" icon, so I poke through the options, thinking I must have done something wrong. Every hour, or so, I go back to the thermostat and try again. Still no heat. I pull a fleece vest over my sweater. By late-afternoon, I'm also wearing my winter coat.

There's a gas fireplace in the living room. It's controlled by a separate thermostat, which I *am* smart enough to operate. When I raise the temperature on that thermostat, flames immediately appear, and the glass door begins to warm. The nearest place to sit is about twelve feet from the fireplace, but it'll be much warmer there than at the kitchen counter on the other side of this long great room. I grab my laptop and settle onto the couch.

This turns out to be a brilliant move. When I sit on the couch with my computer on my lap, Jasmine jumps up and curls her body next to my leg. She doesn't try to climb on me. Hallelujah! She seems content with the side of my thigh. Why didn't I think of this before? Krista ambles over and flops down next to my feet. The dogs are happy. I am happy. We're all content together for an hour or so.

But then, I become aware of a weird smell in the room—a slight tang of metal mixed with something more earthy—and then I hear weird popping noises. Suddenly, a piece of the white ornamental rock surrounding the edges of the fireplace shoots off the wall and lands on the area rug. *WTH!*

I quickly jump up and kick the hot rock off the carpet and onto the entryway tile. Then I rush over and stab my finger at the down arrow on the fireplace thermostat until I hear a click and the gas turns off. The metal and glass on the front of the fireplace are blazing hot—hot enough to launch rocks into the room, apparently. The temperature was set at sixty-eight degrees, but the fireplace, likely added as an aesthetic choice, not a functional heater, stayed on because the temperature never reached sixty-eight degrees in this vast room. My mistake. Most of the heat is probably hovering near the top of the twenty-foot ceiling.

Argh! Why can't I just have a normal, quiet workday for once? Why does nearly every day involve home or pet emergencies or the need for me to figure out something unfamiliar and complicated? Well, that's not a difficult question to answer: because I'm always somewhere new. Unfamiliar environments and situations require extra thinking, which is why most people keep to familiar routines.

Fortunately, this is my last day with Jasmine and Krista in this cavernous, un-cozy, uncomfortable house. All I have to do is get through this evening, tonight, and tomorrow morning.

After I leave here, unfortunately, I'll only have one full day in my cozy little condo and two nights to sleep in my own comfy bed before my next critter sitter job begins: three weeks with Patrick. After Patrick, I'm scheduled to take care of two dogs that (I know from previous experiences) are more challenging than the Irish Setters. I really, really, really don't want to do that job. But I have their deposit money, which I really, really, really don't want to give back. And, of course, they'd never find another critter sitter at the last minute. My conscience won't let me cancel.

■ ■ ■

The next morning, before I leave Jasmine and Krista, I send a text to the woman who hired me: *All went well, except for the heat in the house. I didn't figure that out. But blankets were helpful* [smiling face emoji]

I don't tell her about my problems with Jasmine, or the fireplace rock-popping incident. I just hope the hot-metal smell will have cleared out of the living room by the time they return.

She replies: *Oh! That's terrible. I wish we had known—we would have sent the service guy over!!! I'm so sorry!*

Wait. What?

It takes a minute for me to process the fact that a "service guy" was immediately available to deal with the problem. I thought *I* was doing something wrong when I tried to change the settings on the thermostat—a device that looks like it should be attached to a gadget running the International Space Station.

A tech guy I used to work with threw the words "operator error" at every problem. Sometimes he was correct, and sometimes a glitch in the technology was the actual problem. But he and the adults in my early life conditioned me to assume that whatever went wrong, with anything or anyone, was my fault. But this time the malfunction had nothing to do with me. As always happens with this type of realization, it takes a while for me to accept this as truth.

A few hours after they arrive home, the woman sends me another text: *The furnace guy just left. There was no heat at all. You poor thing, I'm so sorry!*

I reply: *It wasn't a big problem. Glad you got it fixed!*

A positive attitude is always good for business.

It really wasn't a "big" problem. I didn't lie to her or present a false, cheery attitude. My reactions to the conditions I encounter in other people's houses, and with their pets, are mine to own and deal with. I try not to project my personal demons. No one is making me do this work. It's my choice. But is it a choice I'll continue to make?

A few days later, I receive another text message from her. She wants to know if she can book me for several future dates, one of which is five months away. She and her husband have many places to go.

I read and re-read her message. I lay my phone down and stare out the nearest window for a long while. I'm staying with Patrick, who still has no fence around his yard. We've been walking through snow and across icy sidewalks four times a day for the past week. I'm afraid of falling if he spots another dog and goes crazy. My nose is stuffy. I bought an expensive bottle of decongestant spray, which has helped a little, but sometimes I feel like I can't get enough air into my lungs. I might be developing an allergy to some types of dog dander. I'm not sure I'm a good fit for the needs of a King Charles Spaniel.

I pace. I ponder. I dither. I procrastinate.

Two hours later, I reply: Sorry, but I'm not available for any of those dates. Maybe Dana can help.

CHAPTER TWENTY

Looking for Home

I hope reincarnation is real because I'd like another chance at stability. In my next life, I see myself ensconced primarily in one house in one city or town. I see myself as part of a close-knit family. I see myself spending more time writing books and music instead of packing, unpacking, and re-orienting myself to new circumstances every few days, weeks, months, or years. We all want what we don't have, yes? But I think I could do better next time.

As we've established, staying in one place—house, condo, apartment, city, state (other than Montana)—is not one of my skills. But I'd like to believe I still have time to hone that skill, in the right circumstances and with the right person(s).

I dream of sharing a beautiful house with someone, preferably a lead guitar player who enjoys long walks at sunset on the beach and gazes at me adoringly. We'd play in a band together. We'd hike and bike together. We'd have a grand piano in the living room. We'd host wonderful dinner parties and monthly music and poetry salons. Saccharine sigh.

Or maybe I could live with a gaggle of girlfriends and sisters in a collection of small houses surrounding a large common building. The common building would include a communal kitchen and a dining area where we'd all gather for evening meals and conversations. I like the idea of having my own private space while also living with other people. I enjoy other people, but I don't want to be with them every minute of every day. Does anybody want to be with other people every minute of every day? My introverted self certainly doesn't. But maybe I don't need a whole house, small or otherwise, to myself. Perhaps just an office space with a door. Because, really, co-habitation is my preference. Or at least I think it is. I don't really know because I've seldom had that experience (roommates don't count). Am I, once again, looking at the greener grass in someone else's pasture, and thinking I'll like it better over there? Probably so.

On the other hand, my life adventures have contributed depth and richness to my creativity—to my writing and music and visual compositions. My adventures also provide me with stories. The stories in this book, for instance.

Adventure calls to me, with a very loud voice, nearly every day. She cajoles and coerces, telling me about all the shiny, new fun we could have. All I need to do is pack my stuff and follow her lead. But what if I just said NO? What if I found a balance between new experiences and a permanent residence? Surely, there's plenty of veracity in smaller, quieter stories. Not every truthy reveal must come from a life-changing quest, right? Yes. I want to agree. But do I?

In my next life, I will also establish a lucrative career path to support my creative projects. Hmmm…that would leave very little time for working on my creative projects, which is why I've made certain choices during *this* life.

Okay. Well, I still hope reincarnation is true, so I'll have the chance for a do-over.

But wait. Is this desire for a successive life more of the same—another aspect of my constant craving for new experiences?

The inside of my brain is a torture chamber.

Squirrel!

CHAPTER TWENTY-ONE

Betty and Cinder: Anxiety and Joy

Dana needs my help. She's received a last-minute request from one of her best clients. They suddenly need to be out of town for two weekends this month—a family thing—and, of course, Dana is already booked. She tells me it's "really good money." In fact, the amount her clients have offered is nearly twice the daily rate I've been charging.

"What are the dates?" I ask. "Do they have a fenced yard?"

By chance, I'm available for both weekends—mostly because I've been turning down requests from my clients. Dana tells me there's no fenced yard, but the house is on fifteen acres of land.

"It's a beautiful, quiet place," she says, "and the dogs are easy keepers."

"What kind of dogs?"

"A super sweet spaniel and a fearful Mini Aussie."

I've never been around a Mini, but I've known several full-size Australian Shepherd dogs. So I know they are quite intelligent and have strong herding instincts. One of my friends had an Australian Shepherd that used to jump the fence in her back yard and run over to Burke Park. Her dog was captured by Animal Control several times, and taken to doggie jail. The last time she showed up to pay the fine, the complaint stated that her dog had been "nipping at joggers' heels."

A "fearful" Aussie, though? That sounds slightly ominous. But I've soothed many fearful dogs over the years. It should be fine. Still, I hesitate before telling Dana, "Yes, I'll do it."

■ ■ ■

The house isn't completely finished. Two construction vehicles are parked at the top of the driveway alongside a small pickup truck with a snowplow blade attached to the front. The couple and their teenage daughter have only been living there for a few weeks. Two feet of snow cover their fifteen acres of land, as well as the flat roofs of the house, garage, and guest house. Why would architectural designs include flat rooftops in big snow country? This is the Rocky Mountains, where the weight of heavy snow sometimes causes roofs to collapse!

The Friday afternoon I arrive, however, it's warm. Nearly fifty degrees. The snow is melting. Bare ground shows in a few places on the property and I can see that the landscaping hasn't been finished. There are patches of mud in the yard near the house, and the driveway is a soupy brown mess. Dogs and mud are a very bad combination. I hope these people have lots of old towels.

With most dogs, wiping their feet is not a problem when they come back into the house. Many dogs I've cared for are so used to it that they lift their feet for me. But right away I can see it's going to be a problem here. The "fearful" Aussie, Betty, won't let me get near her. The moment I open the door of her crate, she runs to the other end of this three-million-dollar house. (That price tag came up during Dana's conversation with the owners, when the man told her he'd had trouble getting contractors to fix mistakes they'd made—like installing metal countertops in the kitchen instead of the concrete countertops indicated in the design plans. "Even when you've paid three million to have a house built," he said, "contractors will still ignore you." This is proof that no amount of money can over-come the current labor shortage in Bozeman.)

When I walk through the kitchen area of the great room, Betty plays keep-away with me. She hides on the opposite side of the island counter, barking and growling and popping up to see where I am like she's part of a whack-a-mole game. Dana told me to expect this behavior for a while. "Just ignore her," she said, "until she gets used to you."

So that's what I'm doing. But I wonder how I'll be able to wipe Betty's muddy feet after she's been outside since I can't get within six feet of her. I soon realize, however, that wiping her muddy feet won't be a concern. Not until I can get her to *go* outside, anyway.

In stark contrast, Cinder, the Cocker Spaniel, is a lover and a delight. She follows me around the house as I get settled into the guest room. She offers empathy and support as I try to figure out how to turn on the cooktop in the kitchen. It's a sheet of black glass. The word "Gaggenau" is printed in tasteful silver letters on the front piece. A Google search reveals that this stovetop is "the world's preeminent brand of restaurant-grade cooking technology for the modern home." From a YouTube video, I learn that the cooktop includes a child lock safety feature. No wonder.

From the number of instructional videos available online, I surmise that other people have also had trouble operating a cooktop without knobs or other apparent controls. Turns out, I must press a certain spot on the bottom left side of a nearly invisible black rectangle (located on the black glass) for exactly three seconds to activate a heretofore invisible settings panel. From there, I need to figure out which icon to press to accomplish my goal of boiling water for tea or heating soup. I vow to bring my own electric kettle the next time I stay here.

The refrigerator, dishwasher, and trash containers are also invisible in this kitchen. They all look like cabinets. Every surface is smooth and sleek. Unless you count the ultra-modern low-backed, white couches, there's not a spec of cozy anywhere inside these rooms made of metal, concrete, and glass.

The views from inside this house are wonderful, though. Three of the four walls are floor-to-ceiling glass, either windows or doors. Groves of Aspen and pine trees almost appear to be inside the room with me. And, as Dana said, it's very quiet, except for the occasional burst of rattling bugle calls of the sandhill cranes strutting around on a hill above the driveway.

Even though I'm afraid of muddy dog feet (white couches!), I'm glad it's warm and sunny. The back patio area of this house faces south, so the concrete pavers have been soaking up sunshine for hours by the time I arrive on Friday afternoon.

After I haul my stuff inside and get oriented, I open one of the (many) glass doors in the great room. Cinder rushes over and runs outside, grabbing a florescent orange tennis ball on her way past the enormous outdoor grill. In the meantime, Betty cowers as far away from me as she can

"Suit yourself," I say to her with a shrug. "Your loss. We're going out to have some fun." I step outside, leaving the door open.

I'm happy to see that there's only one patch of bare ground in the back yard, which is not a yard at all. It's about fourteen acres of meadow and lightly forested land. Wildlife habitat. On my way to this house, I drove past dozens of deer sauntering beside the road. Dozens more grazed in yards and on hillsides. Several deer congregated on a circle of asphalt where the road ends and the driveway to this house begins to slope downhill. (Normally, in a subdivision, I'd call the road a street, but here the word "road" seems like a better descriptor. I drove through the subdivision for more than a mile and a half, at twenty-five miles per hour, to get to the driveway.)

I can't see what's under the snow, but, having hiked through mountainous terrain since childhood, I recognize the shape of the land. It's a low, boggy meadow tucked under the northern end of the Gallatin Mountains. It's a place that collects and hoards water, so it'll be available for plants, animals, and clouds during the hottest weeks of summer. It is not a place for a house. But I'm happy to see that most of these acres will remain in their natural state. The contractor carved out a building site on less than an acre at the bottom of the hill. The garages are attached to the house, and the guest house is on the other side of the driveway. So, most of the land was not disturbed.

The upside to having lots of money is that you can buy land and then let the plants, birds, and animals continue living there—assuming they stick around during the trauma of construction and adapt to the constant presence of people and vehicles. I can easily imagine these acres continuing to support wildlife. What I could never have imagined is the thing I'm looking at now: an uncovered outdoor lap pool!

Stretching between the concrete paving stones of the patio and the snow-covered meadow is a long metal rectangle filled with water. I estimate the tank to be around twenty-five feet long and eight feet wide. Invisible jets create a gentle current inside the tank. There's a wide ledge at one end of the pool—a place for a person to step or sit on before sliding into the water. I step onto that ledge and bend down to dip my fingers into the water. It's warm, but not hot. I'm not at all tempted to take my clothes off and go for a swim.

My mind turns to the practical. The cost of heating the water in this metal tank must be, well, astronomical. I wonder where the water comes from. Is this subdivision, located several miles from downtown Bozeman, connected to city water?

Surely not. Each piece of property must have its own well. Of course. I push away thoughts about the impacts of residential development on ground water and aquifer resources in the Gallatin Valley. I have other things to think about right now.

My biggest concern for the rest of this weekend is how to care for a dog that won't let me near her. I step up from the lap pool ledge and onto the patio. I glance back toward the house. Betty is standing in the open doorway, looking directly at me.

"Hey, you," I say. "Wanna come out and play?" She doesn't move.

I glance out across the expanse of whiteness to locate Cinder. She's easy to spot in her black and gray coat. She's on her back in the snow, wriggling from side to side, thoroughly enjoying her moment in the sun. Such an exuberant display of dog joy.

"Cinder!" I call to her, "Where's your ball?" She jumps to her feet, lifts her head toward me. She leaps through the deep snow, plows around until she finds the tennis ball, grabs it, bounds up the steps, and drops it at my feet. I bounce it off the pavers and out into the field.

The orange ball disappears into the white snow. Cinder zigs and zags across the snow-covered field, snuffling and digging until she uncovers the ball. Hunting genes are strong in this dog. The Cocker Spaniels I've encountered have all been cheerful, playful dogs. But Cinder might be the most cheerful, playful dog of them all. She oozes joy and affection, even though her people are gone, and she's only known me for fifteen minutes. I like this dog. I like her so much that I momentarily contemplate adopting a Cocker Spaniel of my own. Momentarily.

I look over at the house and notice that Betty has ventured out through the doorway and onto the patio. Normally, I would say "Come on out and play!" but I remember Dana's advice to ignore her and turn my attention back to Cinder and the tennis ball. After I throw the ball a few more times, I look around and see that Betty has moved to the middle of the patio. She's watching us. This time I can't help myself.

"Good girl," I say, a bit too loudly. "Wanna play?" Immediately, Betty sprints in the opposite direction. She races along the back of the house, around the corner, and out of sight.

That would be a No, then. Good grief! How will I get her back into the house? But apparently Betty is more afraid of being outside alone than she is of me. Cinder and I walk through the house and out into the garage, where I press the opener for one of the two overhead doors. The garage connects to the laundry room, so I leave that door open, too. It's a good thing it's relatively warm outside so I can leave doors open everywhere. If it were ten degrees, like last week, this would be a different configuration of problems.

One of the cabinets inside the laundry room—a room twice the size of the master suite in my condo—is crammed full of dog food and several bags of treats. I pull out a bag that proudly announces its contents as "Bovine Tripe" and "100% Pure" with no gluten or grain. Cinder trots over and sits next to me, swishing her hairy tail across the floor and looking at me with huge, irresistible brown eyes. I open the bag and peer inside. The Bovine Tripe looks disgusting, but it must taste great. Cinder is vibrating, eager to get some into her mouth. I hand her a small piece. She quickly gulps it down and waits for more.

"Okay," I say, laughing and pawing through the bag to find the biggest chunk.

While Cinder chews her tripe I walk outside, crinkling the sturdy plastic bag (the universal sound of impending treats these days), and call for Betty. I'm relieved when I see her at the top of the driveway: a small long-haired, tan-and-white dog standing on a dark muddy roadway with white snow piled high on either side of it—a little dog silhouetted against a wide cloudless blue sky, like a long shot in a movie.

"Betty. Come!" I shout into the crisp air, shivering, trying not to sound impatient. It is not warm on the shady side of the garage. Betty remains motionless, but looks down at me. That's encouraging. I soften my tone. "Come on, I've got treats for you!" I crinkle the bag. Betty turns her head to look behind her and then back to me, considering. I crinkle the bag again, as loudly as possible. She doesn't move. Aarrgh. I turn and walk toward the open garage door. I need my jacket.

Inside the laundry room, Cinder does a fancy dance, tail feathers waving, waiting for more tripe. "No," I tell her. "You've had enough." I don't know anything about the effects of bovine tripe on canine digestive systems. Images of black diarrhea staining wool area rugs and clinging to the back sides of long-haired dogs flash through my mind. No, nope, huh-uh. Not doing that. "No more treats for you, Cinder. It'll be time for dinner soon. You can wait." She looks like she could wait for several days. She's not a slender girl.

I grab my jacket off a wooden peg—one of a dozen lined up on the wall next to the door—and pull it on. But then, just as I'm ready to go outside, I look over and see Betty inside the garage, standing next to a jumble of patio furniture. Yay! I lean down and grab Cinder's collar with my left hand and hold onto her. I reach into the bag with my right hand, find two small pieces of tripe, and toss one toward the open laundry room door. I pull Cinder with me as I back into the hallway leading to the kitchen. Once we're in the hallway, I throw another piece of tripe. It lands in the middle of the laundry room floor.

My tricks work. While Betty is busy eating her tripe inside the laundry room, I hurry to the front door and jog around to the garage to press the button that closes the overhead door. When she hears the garage door closing, Betty scurries down the hallway and into the kitchen. Now all I have to do is trick her into eating. Dana warned me that she might go on a hunger strike.

Betty won't come near me for the rest of the day, most of which she spends cowering between chair legs under the dining table. She eats her dinner, though, after I slide the bowl into her safe space under one of the chairs. So, no hunger strike after all. She also eats a few treats, although I have to throw them on the floor and walk to the far side of the room before she'll creep forward eight inches to snap them up. Except for Betty's occasional outbursts of barking and growling, the dogs and I enjoy a quiet evening in the house. I read. Cinder lounges next to me on the couch. Betty alternates between a wary stance of vigilance under the table and bouts of vigorous yapping.

At bedtime, I leave the door to the patio standing open and tell the dogs to "go potty"—hoping it's a command they recognize. Cinder immediately runs out, squats in the snow, and runs back inside. But Betty cowers and growls at me. After about fifteen minutes of trying to coax her outside with a trail of treats on the floor, I give up. I leave the door open while I go into the guest room to get ready for bed. When I walk back into the great room later, Betty is still under the table. If she won't walk through an open door and I can't get close enough to clip a leash onto her collar and lead her outside, I'm not sure what to do.

So, I do nothing except hope she has a strong bladder.

■ ■ ■

The next morning, the house feels cold. Much too cold. After a short investigation, I find the source of the frigid air: the laundry room, where the outside door is standing open. I'm not sure how long the door has been open. I know it was shut when I went to bed. This is weird. Betty is the logical culprit, but she is a Mini Aussie, a very small dog. She isn't more than thirteen or fourteen inches high. I can't figure out how she could open the door, but there's no other explanation. She must be a skilled jumper.

A text exchange with Dana confirms my suspicions.

Me: *The laundry room door was standing open when I got up this morning. Not sure if Betty did that. Doesn't seem like she's tall enough. No wind last night or this morning.*

Dana: *Oh shoot that is Betty!*

Me: *Well, it's nice to know she can let herself out instead of pooping in the house* [grimace emoji]

Dana: *I would lock her in the outside kennel with Cinder for a while in the evening before bed. She knows how to use that space.*

Good to know.

After breakfast, I settle onto one of the couches in the great room to read for a while. Cinder jumps up beside me. I've been told that these dogs have couch and bed privileges. There are a few muddy paw prints on the white couches in front of the fireplace, but I'll wait until I'm about to leave to wash those off. No sense cleaning couches more than once. Cinder snores lightly while I read essays about motorcycles written by Lily Brooks-Dalton.

Later, when I get up to stretch, I step out into the front entryway and see that the door to the guest house is also standing open. There are streaks of mud on the door, evidence that Betty jumped up on it to push the lever handle down. After I walk across the driveway to close it, I see the door to the gym, which is on the lower level of the guest house, standing open, too. That door is also streaked with dried mud. The gym is where Betty's people work out. It's obvious she went there early this morning looking for them. Betty may be small, but she is smart and determined.

■ ■ ■

The Bozeman Ukulele Society is hosting a sing-along at the mall at noon today, and I volunteered to help lead some of the songs. At 11:30 I call the dogs and tell them to get into their crates in the master bedroom. Cinder immediately trots down the hallway and ducks into her crate, but Betty has resumed her cowering position under the dining table. This is unexpected because, this morning while I read, she ventured over several times and sat on the floor next to my feet. She had even let me pet her for a few seconds. I thought she finally trusted me, that we had moved beyond her fearful behavior. But no.

I find a bag of very tiny treats in the laundry room cabinet and create a line of them across the floor. The trail of treats leads from the great room, down the hallway, into the master suite, and into Betty's crate. That done, I hide in the master closet with the door open just wide enough to see Betty. I plan to sneak into the hallway behind her and close the door. Then, she'll be in the bedroom with nowhere else to go, except into her crate. It's a good plan. But Betty is cautious.

She creeps forward and then carefully eats one treat while glancing around fearfully. She stands motionless for several minutes before inching forward to the next treat. From inside the closet, I watch her, and the time, creeping forward. I fret and fume. By the time Betty is done walking down the hallway and into her crate, it's noon. It'll take me twenty-five minutes to drive to the mall from here. The sing-along will be half over by the time I get there. I hate being late. I hate reneging on my commitments. But I don't go to the mall.

Instead, I drive into town and order a toasted bagel from the drive-through attendant at Freshies Café. The bagel is slathered with cream cheese and topped with slices of avocado and bacon. I also buy a large bottle of sugary ginger ale. It's been less than two hours since I ate breakfast. I'm not hungry. I don't need this food. But I eat it anyway, sitting inside my small SUV, in the parking lot, while mentally chastising myself for this bad behavior that I don't want to do but can't seem to stop. Anxiety eating is my nemesis.

■ ■ ■

That evening I use the trail of treats trick again. This time, I'm trying to get Betty into the outdoor kennel to pee before bedtime, as Dana suggested. The outdoor kennel is a small area behind the back wall of the garage that's surrounded by a chain-link fence. I don't want to let Cinder and Betty (not that she'd go) out into the unfenced acres around the house because deer have been walking through the field all evening. There's been a lot of barking in the house during the past hour. I'm afraid the dogs will run off in pursuit of a whitetail, and I won't be able to find them in the dark. Dana cautioned me about the possibility of them chasing deer, and I don't want to risk that.

It takes about forty-five minutes to coax Betty through the laundry room and garage, and into the outdoor kennel. She plays hide and seek with me in the garage, cowering and shaking behind patio furniture, boxes, and various tools and pieces of equipment. Once she finally darts through the door and into the snow-covered kennel, I wait another twenty minutes while she doesn't pee. I watch surreptitiously through the glass window in the door, because I prefer to see dogs pee before

I go to sleep. It's good for my peace of mind. Several times, I open the door and say, "go potty," which I have confirmed—with both Dana and the man who lives in this house—is a command both dogs understand. Cinder pees right away, but Betty stands next to the fence with her nose in the air, sniffing intently, *not* peeing. During those twenty minutes, poor Cinder faces the door, waiting, ready for bed. I'm afraid to let her in, though, because Betty will come in, too, and she hasn't peed.

But I finally give up and let them inside. "You'd better not pee in the house," I tell Betty. "And I'm locking the doors." She scuttles inside, runs into the entertainment room, and huddles against the couch in the farthest corner. I lock all the doors with the dead bolts before crawling into bed.

■ ■ ■

The next morning, I check the floors, rugs, and furniture inside the house. There are no puddles or piles. Whew! Betty must have a super-dog bladder. As far as I know, she hasn't peed since mid-afternoon yesterday.

In the laundry room, I fill both bowls with food. Cinder prances in, quickly eats everything in her bowl, and begins to eye Betty's food. Meanwhile, Betty stands in the hallway, watching me and Cinder but not coming inside. I move across the room and sit on the bench near the outside door, underneath the coat pegs, and call Cinder to me. She trots right over, eager for some petting. I focus on Cinder, keeping my head down, ignoring Betty completely.

Soon, in my peripheral vision, I see Betty take a few hesitant steps toward her bowl. I stay as still as possible while continuing to stroke Cinder and cooing nonsense into her ears: "Who's the best dog in the house? That's right. It's you. You're a good girl, not like that fraidy cat Betty. What a good girl you are!" Betty creeps forward until she's inside the room with us. She glances at her food bowl and then looks over at me and Cinder, takes another step. I ignore her.

Eventually, Betty makes it across the room to her bowl and eats, perhaps ready for a slice of normal after eating three meals under the dining table. In a few hours, Dana will be here to stay with the dogs until their people return late this evening. So, I'm done with mealtimes. Yay! My remaining worry is how I'll get Betty into her crate when I'm ready to leave.

After she eats, Betty walks over and leans against my leg, next to Cinder, and lets me pet her. She must be desperate for attention. She comes to me several more times during the morning and early afternoon. Since I'm the only human available, I guess she's decided that affection from me is better than no affection. As long as I sit, and don't move anything except an arm, she's friendly. Whenever I stand up, however, she barks, growls, and runs away. Thankfully, I'll be out of here soon and Dana can deal with Betty.

When it's almost time for me to leave the house, Betty surprises me. I tell her to get into her crate—giving myself an extra thirty minutes to accomplish the task—and she scampers down the hallway without any treat trail, coaxing or shenanigans. She sprints across the bedroom and straight into the crate. I'm not sure what I've done right, but I'll take the win. This makes me feel better about the next weekend that I'm scheduled to be with Betty and Cinder.

■ ■ ■

A few days before the second gig, Dana and I talk about how to make things easier—for me and for Betty. She consulted with the owners who gave me the option of staying in the guest house. It's smaller than the main house and we all decided it would be an easier space in which to control Betty. We also made that decision because of the white couches. The yard and driveway are an even bigger muddy mess these days. Every time the dogs go outside, they'll return with dirty feet and bellies. There's no possibility of keeping the white couches in the house clean unless I can wipe Betty down with a towel. And there's no way for me to do that unless I can get close to her. So, before they leave for their trip, the people carry the large, heavy, high-end wooden dog crates across the driveway and up the stairs to the great room in the guest house. I arrive a few hours later.

After I park in the driveway and walk up the stairs to the guesthouse, I approach the crates to let the dogs out, greeting them with my best non-threatening voice. But Betty immediately begins to growl and bark.

"It's okay, Betty. Remember me? I'm your friend," I coo as I let Cinder out and pet her for a minute. Cinder wriggles and licks my hand, happy to see me. But, when I open Betty's crate, she snarls and snaps her teeth at me. I pull my hand away just in time to avoid her sharp little teeth connecting with my fingers. At the same time, I instinctively lean away from her, which gives Betty an opening. She dashes out of the crate, runs down the stairs, jumps up and opens the outside door, sprints across the driveway to the main house, where she opens the laundry room door and runs inside, spreading muddy footprints across the floors.

Luckily (for me), Dana decided to meet me at the house—to be sure everything was okay with this new setup. She drives up in time to see Betty streak across the driveway with me in pursuit.

Dana jumps out of her pickup truck and yells, "I'll get her."

I'm very happy to see Dana. I need a minute to recover from nearly being bitten. Dana is not so lucky, though. Betty snaps at her, sinking teeth into the skin of her hand far enough to draw blood.

After a series of strategic maneuvers, in which Dana and I block Betty's access to the large rooms in the main house, we finally corral her in a corner of the laundry room. Dana clips a leash to Betty's collar. We walk over to the guest house, wipe muddy paws, and sit down on the couch, which is dark gray, not white—another reason for this accommodation decision—so we can talk about how to get through this weekend. Dana offers to trade jobs with me, but I decline. She's staying with a dog that's dying of cancer. The situation sounds complicated. The dog is anxious and needs to be tricked into taking medications several times each day. No thanks. The last thing that poor dog needs is an unfamiliar caregiver in his house.

Dana and I wonder why a person would leave a pet that's so sick. But then we wonder a lot of things about people and their pets. For instance, how did Betty's behavior get so out of control, literally, and why won't these people do something about it? The woman who lives in this house is the only person Betty will obey, making our job very difficult. Even the woman's husband can't control Betty.

We decide to leave a leash attached to Betty's collar all weekend. She'll just have to drag it around the guest house, day and night. It's a six-foot leash, so I can easily grab the end of it without getting near her teeth. With a leash on her, I'll be able to walk Betty up the driveway to the paved road, where it's not so muddy. If she doesn't pee while we're walking, I'll put her into the outdoor kennel and leave her there for a while. I'll also be able to pull her over to her crate and coax her inside with treats when I need to leave. It's the best plan we can come up with to keep both me and Betty safe.

As we talk, Betty sits on the couch next to Dana. Every time I speak or move an arm, she growls and barks at me. Her voice is menacing, a stark contrast to her sweet little face and body. Dana gives the leash a quick upward jerk and tells her to Knock it off! But Betty continues expressing her displeasure at my presence, acting like I'm dog enemy number one. I'll get through this weekend, somehow, because I promised Dana I would. But that's it.

"I won't take care of this dog again," I say to her. She replies with a silent nod. What can she say, really? She understands that I am completely serious.

CHAPTER TWENTY-TWO

Terrible News

The number on my screen belongs to the woman who's cat I'm scheduled to take care of next week. The text delivers terrible news: Her cat, Missy, died yesterday.

The news is terrible for three reasons. First, Missy's person is upset. She loved that cat who'd been with her for more than sixteen years. I like Missy's person. I feel her pain.

Second, it reminds me of the deaths of my sister's cats, Bosley and Maisie.

Third, any pet's death reminds me of when I lost the canine love-of-my-life, MooJee. MooJee, a mix of black Labrador Retriever and Golden Retriever, refused to retrieve anything. Ever. Each time I threw a ball or a stick, she looked at me like I was crazy. I could hear her thinking, *If I go get that ball and bring it to you, you'll just throw it again and I'll have to go get it again. It will never end.* She was a smart dog and highly bored by repetitive activities. We understood each other well.

MooJee and I shared adventures across Montana for fifteen years. We hiked and cross-country skied, floated rivers in rafts and canoes, and swam in streams, ponds, and lakes. MooJee loved water. And she loved being with me. She even came onstage during a few of my band gigs at Chico Hot Springs and outdoor wedding receptions. Even now, twelve years later, I can hardly imagine sharing my life with any other dog. Although I often think about it.

After she died, the box that contained MooJee's ashes traveled with me in my car for several months. One day, when I finally felt able to let go of them, I drove to a place where huge slabs of orange-red rock sloped down into a wide spot along the Clark Fork River. It was a windless, sunny autumn day—perfect weather for tossing ashes. Dried grasses and a few cottonwood trees wearing a mix of gold and green leaves bordered the river. I held the box carefully as I side-stepped down the slope of rock to the water. A bank of white clouds hovering above the Bitterroot Mountains witnessed an extemporaneous eulogy to my wonderful companion and exemplary dog. And then I let the river carry her ashes from Alberton, Montana, to Lake Pend Oreille, into the Columbia River, and on out to the Pacific Ocean. (Well, I like to think that at least a few particles of her ashes made it past the more than four hundred and seventy dams blocking that watershed.)

I'm sure Missy's person felt the same intense connection to and love for her cat. And this is not about me.

I reply to Missy's person with a heart-felt message of con-
dolence and an offer to listen. The next day, I take a bottle of
cabernet sauvignon to her house. We open the wine, pour, and
toast to Missy, to the love this beautiful feline companion gave
her person throughout her long kitty life.

CHAPTER TWENTY-THREE

Billie and Cleaver: Destroying Christmas

Day One:
I glance up from my laptop and look around. Something doesn't sound right. Both dogs are lying on a rug in the living room. From where I sit, I can see the floor around them strewn with bones: plastic bones, nylon bones, and actual animal leg bones. There's also a thick braid of rope and a mangled cloth fish. Ten minutes ago, the dogs pulled all their toys and bones out of a wicker basket, and then chased after each other for a while before settling down to gnaw on their chosen bone. Or so I thought.

I lean forward, looking for the source of that weird little noise. I'm sitting at the dining room table where I've been editing a podcast episode for a client. From here I can see dog butts, but not what they're chewing on. What is that sound?

I stand up and walk into the living room half of this great room. Just past the massive leather-topped coffee table, I stop, and then gasp in horror. Tiny slivers of wood litter the floor, along with several half-chewed ornaments. I glance over at the Christmas tree standing near the front door. The bottom branches are bare. A few minutes ago, those branches were crowded with ornaments—ornaments with fly fishing and hunting scenes stamped on them. Expensive and unique ornaments. Now, the lower branches of the tree are bare.

"What the heck!" I yell.

Billie, the one-year-old German Wirehair Pointer sprawled on the area rug, stops biting at the ornament she's holding between her paws. She looks up at me with an expression of pure innocence.

The other dog, a large, fluffy black Bernedoodle with two white feet, stops chewing on his bone and lifts his head. He needs to know what's wrong so he can adjust his behavior to please. His name, Cleaver, is crazily appropriate. He's the definition of a companion dog. A dog that always wants to be near, or sitting on, his people. Always. He cleaves.

Cleaver hurries over to lean his big head against my thigh. I give him a quick reassuring pat before pushing Billie away from the mess and kneeling to evaluate the damage.

I thought the noises I heard in the background as I worked came from both dogs gnawing on bones—until that odd little crunching sound caught my attention. Now it's obvious that Billie ignored everything from the toy basket in favor of what hung on the Christmas tree. She has used her needle-like teeth to chew the ornaments into tiny fragments of wood.

I crawl across the rug, separating slivers of wood from the wool fibers and gathering splinters from under the coffee table. Billie hops up on one of the leather couches. She waits patiently for me to finish so she can get back to her chewing. I've never seen her so calm. Why is she so calm? Once my hand is full of damaged ornaments, I stand up and think about what to do with the debris. Billie jumps down from the couch and presses her nose against my hand, wiggling and wagging. Now she's not so calm. She wants to get her teeth back into those ornaments.

"No!" I say firmly, pointing to the other end of the room. "Go away." Billie briefly contemplates this command before bounding away, back toward the Christmas tree where more tasty ornaments hang within her reach. "No Billie!" I shout. This time she makes the correct decision and retreats to the dining room.

My mind returns to the dilemma of what to do with the stuff in my hand. Sure, I could throw the pieces into the trash. But after serious consideration, I choose not to do that. Instead, I preserve the evidence.

There's a bookshelf near the Christmas tree. I shove books aside to make space for the fragments. I remove all the other wooden ornaments from the low tree branches and set them on the bookshelf, too. I take a picture of the mess with my phone and send it to the wife of the couple who hired me to take care of their dogs, along with a message: *Billie is eating the Christmas tree ornaments!*

I return to the dining room and sit in front of my laptop. Cleaver follows me to the table and tries to climb onto my lap. After my shouts at Billie, he needs my assurance that he's not in trouble. He's nearly tall enough to eat off the table, so he's not exactly a lap dog. I rub his ears for a while and then gently push him away.

"Good boy, I say, "you're a good boy. Not like that other dog, that bad dog. She's such a bad dog!"

Billie bounds over to get in on the attention. She jumps at my head and licks my face, knocking my glasses askew. "Go away!" I say quietly, pointing my index finger toward the back of the house. Billie bounds across the room in the opposite direction and skids to a stop in front of the Christmas tree. "No!" I yell at her.

Cleaver scampers under the table and wedges as much of his body between my legs as possible. Billie turns to look at me but doesn't move away from the tree. I plant my elbows on the table and press my hands into the sides of my aching head.

I like these dogs. I really do. They are sweet and loving. Their bad behavior is not their fault. When I arrived at this house to talk with the people about the possibility of taking care of their dogs, Billie and Cleaver barked and jumped on me from the moment I walked through the door. When I sat down, the dogs jumped up on the couch and mauled me, licking my face and stabbing their toenails into my legs.

Their people smiled and said, "Oh look, they like you!" At that moment, I should have stood up and walked out the door.

Finally, the man noticed that I needed the mauling to stop. "Get down," he said. Cleaver responded by putting his paws on my shoulders and running his big tongue across the hair on the side of my head (because I had turned my face away from him). Billie jumped down for two seconds and then leaped back onto my lap where, she began furiously digging at my right leg as if she needed to bury a freshly shot sage hen inside my thigh.

The woman said, "I'll show you how to make them behave," and hurried off into another part of the house. She returned with a bowl full of treats. She stuck the bowl under each dog's nose. They jumped off me and began to jump on her. She extended the bowl toward me, and I decided to take charge.

I stood up, bowl of treats in one hand and my other arm stretched out, palm toward the leaping dogs, fingers pointed upward in the universal traffic cop sign for STOP. (Or, if you're old enough to remember this, the gesture all three of The Supremes made while singing, "Stop in the name of love, before you break my heart.") I told the dogs to SIT. They sat. I told them to STAY. They stayed. I said, "Good dogs." I gave them each several treats, but only while they were sitting. If they moved, I turned my back on them until they sat still.

Scenarios such as this get me hired. People with dogs that won't behave are amazed. They think I'm some sort of dog whisperer. I'm not a dog whisperer, but I know this much: Nearly all bad dog behavior is created by bad people behavior. Dogs need to know the rules. And the rules must be consistently enforced so the dogs understand where their boundaries are.

I also know this: Dogs want to please their people. Right now, Cleaver and Billie can sense that I am not pleased. They both stare at me. I decide to take a break from work so we can all go outside for a while.

There's no fence around this property, but beyond the back yard is a huge field that grows alfalfa during the summer. It's covered by two feet of snow. It looks like the perfect place for a romp, a place for them to burn off some of their young-dog energy and get tired enough to take a nap while I finish my work. It's a brilliant idea. I'm so smart!

Before they left, the people told me Billie didn't need to be on a leash. *She'll come back when you call her,* the woman wrote in a text. *But Cleaver needs to be on a leash whenever he's outside the dog run.*

The dog run is a small, fenced area for the dogs to do a quick pee or poop, not a place for them to run and play. The unfenced yard or field is the only option around here for vigorous exercise. I pull my winter boots on, snap a leash to Cleaver's collar, and open the back door. That's when the trouble begins.

Billie takes off like she's been shot out of a cannon. Cleaver lunges after her, yanking me through the deep snow and across the yard. I stumble along as best I can, trying not to fall. We are nearly to the field when Cleaver charges through a stand of dried Bull Thistle.

Every flower and stem on a Bull Thistle plant has a cluster of sharp, sturdy spines attached to it—some of which are very long. It's just about impossible to touch any part of a Bull Thistle plant without getting stabbed, sometimes deep enough to draw blood. The spines attach themselves to everything: gloves, leggings, furry boots, skin, dog hair...whatever they can get their sticky little hands on.

Cleaver begins to bark and hop around like he'd been stabbed with a hot poker—because he probably feels like he's been stabbed with a hot poker. His fur is dotted with clumps of thistle spikes, including a few near his eyes. My legs, gloves, and coat are covered with thistle heads and spines. Shit!

"Come on Cleaver," I say, yanking on the leash. "Let's go back to the house and get rid of these things." Shortest outdoor adventure, ever.

I yell for Billie. No Billie appears. I yell again. And again. Still no Billie. So much for *she'll come back when you call her.* I drag Cleaver to the back entryway of the house, tell him to sit, and begin pulling thistles off his fur. He squirms and whines. The thistles poke through my gloves and embed themselves into my fingers. Soon, my back starts to ache. I stand up and stretch. I call for Billie again. She doesn't respond. Maybe she's sniffing through the bushes at the edge of the field, ignoring me. Or she's run off. Whatever.

I finally get most of the spines off Cleaver and let him back into the house. I gather all the thistles into a pile and tromp out to the trash container at the end of the driveway. I open the lid and throw them inside. Standing beside the trash container, I pull pieces of thistles off my coat, leggings, and boots and toss those bits in, as well. By the time I've done all that, my gloves are a total loss. It would take hours to pull all the spikes out of them with pliers. And I'd probably stab myself a thousand more times during the process. My fingers already look like my mother's pin cushion. The gloves go into the trash as well.

Inside the house, Cleaver is busy chewing on his fur, trying to get rid of the broken bits of thistle embedded in his skin. I sit down beside him, to help. Suddenly, he starts to cough and spin around in circles. He races through the house. I run after him, try to calm him down. But he keeps spinning around and around, like he's chasing his tail. Except he's not chasing his tail. He's gagging and coughing and making ghastly choking sounds. I realize he must have swallowed some bits of thistle. I dash into the guest room to find my page of notes that includes emergency contact info. My level of panic escalates. What if he chokes to death before I can get him to the vet?

By the time I rush back into the living room, Cleaver has stopped spinning. Now, he's standing in front of the Christmas tree. Biting at it. I watch with dismay as he puts a branch into his mouth, strips it with his teeth, and then chews and swallows the evergreen needles. OMG, what am I going to tell these people about their tree?

I pace around the room, hitting my forehead with the palm of my hand. In more than thirty years of staying with hundreds of pets, this situation has never come up. Nothing even remotely close. I have no idea what to do. Should I drag him away from the tree, carry him to the car, and drive him to the vet? Am I strong enough to pick up a large struggling, panicked dog and carry him across the ice and snow in the driveway without falling and hurting both of us? Probably not. Most definitely not. I should call the vet to get advice. I grab my phone, find the emergency contact info, and start to punch in the number.

But then I stop and watch as Cleaver frantically bites the tree, chews, and swallows. I get it: *He* knows what to do. He instinctively knows that eating pine needles will dislodge the thistle spines stuck in his throat. I just need to let him take care of himself. Okay. Okay. Everything will be fine.

Oh, no! Billie!

I run to the patio door, forgetting to put my coat on, and stumble through the snow calling, "Billie! Billie, where are you? Billie! Come!"

Billie does not come.

I dash back into the house and sprint to the living room. Cleaver is still eating the Christmas tree, but he is standing up and alive. I run back to the patio, grabbing my coat on the way, pulling it on as I rush out the door. No Billie in the yard. I hurry out to the front of the house and look left and right. No Billie anywhere on the street or in the front yards of the neighborhood houses. I run to the back yard again and stop to scan every bush, tree, and rock. German Wirehaired Pointer dogs are the color of fall and winter: a blend of brown, gray, and white. Even if, at this very moment, she was sniffing her way through the hedge of bushes bordering the yard, I probably couldn't see her.

"Billie!" I yell again. "Billie!" Nothing moves anywhere in the yard or the field.

I give up and hurry into the house to check on Cleaver. He's still eating the tree but seems less frantic, which is encouraging. I begin to feel slightly less frantic myself. As I turn to go back outside, through the living room window I see a brown-gray-white shape moving through the row of bushes bordering the yard. Billie! I sprint to the door.

■ ■ ■

Day Two:

Highway traffic and trains are my soundtrack in this house. Traffic noise from I-90 is constant, although it decreases significantly during the night. Noise from the train, however, blares throughout the day and night. About a mile away, a secondary road leading into the Bridger Mountains crosses the train tracks that run parallel to the interstate highway. I've been told that trains are required to blow an air horn—which seems much too mild a phrase for the ear-bashing blast of sound they emit—as they approach any place where tracks cross a road or a street. That requirement is, apparently, in effect 24/7.

Last night I noted every blast: 9:30 p.m., 11 p.m., 12:30 a.m., 1:20 a.m., 4:30 a.m., 5:45 a.m., 6:30 a.m. How does anyone sleep in this house? Especially in this uncomfortable guest room bed. And why, why, why would anyone buy a house so close to the Interstate highway and train tracks?

I am exhausted. But I have a deadline, so I'm sitting at the table editing a series of episodes for the Biographers International podcast. The dogs circle the coffee table and leap at each other in the living room. All the doors to other rooms in the house are closed so I can keep them in sight.

Billie jumps up on a couch, postures, jumps down, and runs behind the coffee table. She peeks out at Cleaver, who is posed in a playful crouch. When he leaps toward her, she runs and jumps onto the other couch. Around and around they go, throwing their young-dog energy all over the room. If the neighborhood's snow packed road wasn't icy, and if they had enough leash manners that I wouldn't need weeks of physical therapy after taking them for a walk…well, scratch that idea. Leash walks are not an option. And I'm certainly not taking them to the field again. But I'm doing my best. So far, they've been outside three times.

First, they went out at 6:30 a.m. for a quick pee and bark-at-the-deer session in the small, fenced dog run outside the laundry room door.

Thirty minutes later, after I'd swallowed a cup of green tea and added a pair of winter leggings to the hoodie I'd slept in (it's really cold in this house, as well as noisy), I put a handful of dog treats into my coat pocket and invited Billie to sniff there. I wanted her to know I had them before I let her out into the big, unfenced yard. She sprinted away, but turned back when I yelled her name and held up a treat. She came back to me, snatched the treat, and then ran off again, but only as far as the hedge of bushes. I turned my attention to Cleaver, who was pulling on the leash attached to his collar.

I stepped on the leash, so he couldn't pull it out of my hand. I clipped his collar to a longer leash—a plastic-coated wire attached to a metal eye-bolt screwed into the side of the house—and then removed the short leash. Cleaver sprinted across the yard until he was yanked back, suddenly, at the end of the wire—a testament to his enthusiasm for chasing Billie, but not a great statement about his intelligence. He's been restricted by this long-leash tether many times and should know how far he can run before reaching the end of it. He doesn't.

I crunched my way across the snow and over next to one of the big trees. I dug through the snow until I found a stick. Cleaver ran over, the long leash rippling behind him. I had to hop around to keep my feet away from the line, to avoid being tripped as he circled me, leaping at the stick. I knew if that line whipped into my ankles I'd be on the ground within a split second. Even if I wasn't injured, it would be difficult to fight my way back into a standing position while wallowing around in deep snow with two dogs jumping all over me.

For about twenty minutes, I threw the stick, dodged the wire, and called Billie back for treats when she got too far away. Each time she returned, she gobbled her treat, leaped at Cleaver a couple of times, and then ran off again. He'd chase her to the end of his long leash, get yanked off his feet, and then bark after her in frustration.

Poor Cleaver. Poor me. But I couldn't think of any other way to get them some exercise. Taking them to a dog park? Out of the question. An option fraught with dangers—to both the dogs and my mental health. Since the sudden influx of new residents and their dogs that began in 2020, when Montana became *The Last Best Place* to get away from COVID-19, the dog parks have become overcrowded and dangerous.

The last time I took other people's dogs to one of the parks, things got ugly after some dog did something that some other dog didn't like. The next day, I drove the dogs to a different park. But we didn't even get out of the car. I took one look at the roiling throng of canines and drove away. The people who hire me don't want to see stitches in their dogs or receive vet bills after they get home.

Cleaver and Billie went out a third time this morning just before I sat down to work. It was another jaunt around the dog run. I scooped their poop off the snow with a garden shovel and stashed it in the five-gallon plastic bucket sitting next to gate. They ran back and forth, chasing each other in between stops to leap at the fence and bark at…everything.

So, yes, now I'm frustrated with their rambunctious rampage around the living room. After three outings in less than two hours, they should be ready for a nap. I certainly am. If only I had some doggie Valium. One of my friends gives her dog anti-anxiety meds whenever she and her husband go on a long road trip. I briefly wonder how I can get my hands on some of those pills? Okay, enough of that. I turn my attention back to the podcast episode I'm editing, to the sound waves displayed on the screen of my laptop. The dogs continue their couch-hopping romp.

The next time I look up to check on them, I see both dogs pulling strings of lights off the Christmas tree.

"NO!" I scream, slamming my knee into the table leg as I jump up. Cleaver and Billie become statue dogs for a nanosecond, and then turn to make another lunge at the tree. "STOP IT!" I yell, followed by a string of blue words after my ankle bone connects with wood as I try to get my long legs out from under the table.

Finally disentangled, I hurry across the room toward them. The dogs peel away from each other and sprint past me, one on my left, one on my right. They think I'm playing keep-away with them. They run back to and around me. They leap onto the couches and onto each other and onto the floor. Up, down, and around.

"COME HERE," I shout, running to grab the treat bag. "TREATS!" But they're apparently not in the mood for treats. They're happy with this fun game of keep-the-dogs-away-from-Chérie. I scrunch the stiff plastic of the treat bag several times. I keep scrunching the bag as I walk toward the back of the house, and they finally stop jumping on each other and run toward me.

I give them each one treat after they obey my command to sit, which seems to break the spell. "Come," I say quietly. They follow me to the laundry room where I open the door to the small fenced area. "GET OUT!" I yell. They are happy to oblige.

Back in the living room, I separate strings of lights from pine needles and decorations on the Christmas tree and move them up to the highest branches. The holiday lights are housed inside bullet casings. The tree decorations are miniature versions of fly-fishing rods, canoes, fish, guns, birds, and bird dogs.

The man who lives in this house told me he grew up in Bozeman. (Anyone who grew up in Bozeman will be sure to mention that fact sometime during the first two minutes of your acquaintance, just so you'll know they aren't a part of the horde of reviled *transplants* around here.) He also told me he left Montana for twenty years and that he and his wife, who's from somewhere in the Midwest, moved back here five years ago.

But even for a guy who grew up fishing and hunting in Montana, and a woman in awe of her manly man from the Wild West, bullet casings on a Christmas tree seems like an odd choice. To me, anyway. In fact, I have to admit that these non-dog-training-murder-weapons-on-the-Christmas-tree people are beyond my ability to understand. As I finish laying the last of the bullet casing lights across the branches at the top of the tree, I remind myself that everyone celebrates the holidays in their own way. And then I flop down into a big armchair.

After I've recovered a bit, I let the dogs into the house. I give them a few more treats and lots of petting. They are calmer now. I am calmer. We snuggle up together on one of the deep, leather couches. Cleaver begins to snore next to my leg. Billie hops over to the other couch and stretches across it on her back, legs in the air.

Once they are both asleep, I ease carefully away from Cleaver and walk over to my laptop. I sit, take a deep breath, and—with the stealth of a parent monitoring a sleeping child in the next room—start working again.

■ ■ ■

Day Five:

There's a chicken coop inside a fenced pen on this property. It sits near the back of the house, maybe twenty feet from the patio door. The fence is eight feet high. The door that opens into the pen is painted a lovely red color. It looks like it should be attached to a house.

I've never opened that door. About a dozen chickens and one tom turkey live here, but I'm not responsible for any of these birds. The people who hired me said to ignore them, which I've done, except to call Billie away from the fence when she terrorizes them with her barking and leaping. There's an automatic food dispenser in the pen, and the water trough is heated. It's a self-sufficient set up, so I don't have any poultry duties. Or rather, I'm not *supposed to* have any poultry duties. Nevertheless, I can't ignore an animal in distress.

I'm about to leave the house when I hear the turkey making unusual noises. I'm familiar with turkey chatter, both wild and domestic, so I know this isn't normal. He sounds upset. I go outside to investigate. The tom paces along the side of the pen that's closest to the house. Back and forth, back and forth. When he sees me, the volume of his chatter increases. He stops pacing and stares at me.

I walk the perimeter of the enclosure, checking the fresh snow on the back side for fox or coyote footprints. There are none. There is nothing on the ground or in the tree branches above the chicken yard that looks alarming. And I need to get to an appointment. I tell the turkey that everything looks fine to me and drive away.

Four hours later, back from appointments and errands, I look out the kitchen window and see a small brown chicken running, frantically, back and forth along the fence. But she's on the wrong side: the outside. She runs past the red door and back to it again, like she wants it to open so she can get inside. She looks freaked out. I don't know much about chickens, but I believe I recognize a chicken that's desperate to get through a door when I see one. I sigh. *You're not responsible for the poultry*, they said. Right.

I step out onto the patio. There are chicken tracks in the fresh snow. It's obvious that the chicken came to the back door. Was she looking for help?

When I walk across the snow toward her, the chicken doesn't run away or even change her behavior. She continues squawking and pacing while I take a video of her squawking and pacing, which I immediately send to the animals' people. While that video is careening through space and satellite beams, aiming for their phones, I open the red door and watch the chicken scurry inside. The turkey lopes over to greet her. He checks her feathers, beak, spikey little claw feet. He inspects the little brown chicken's body thoroughly, emits a few soft turkey sounds, and then returns to his business of being Mister Tom Turkey, Large and In Charge of The Pen.

My phone chimes. It's the wife responding to my chicken video: *Okay. That's weird. Unless there's a break in the fence somewhere. Or she flew* [laughing emoji] *Last week we had an owl get a chicken.*

Again, I carefully check every inch of the poultry yard fence. It is solid. That chicken either flew over the fence or an owl swooped down and carried her off, and then dropped her. Don't know.

When I turn back toward the house, I see Cleaver and Billie watching through the window next to the patio door. They are both vibrating, prancing in place, every muscle aquiver with the need to chase a chicken. Or a turkey. Or a person. Or a stick, Or anything, really. I open the door just wide enough to slide through, pushing them back with my knees as they try to get past my legs and out the door. If only this yard had a fence around it. But sadly, I must disappoint them yet again.

"No," I say. "You can't go out. Sorry."

Some situations simply can't be made any better for a dog, even by an imaginative Super Critter Sitter dubbed "The Dog Whisperer." Reluctantly—after a few more minutes of nose-on-window whining—the dogs accept my decision, and we all go into the living room for couch-cuddle time.

■ ■ ■

It's been nearly four days since Cleaver's and Billie's people returned from their trip, and I still haven't received the money they owe me. My payment policy is to receive half before they leave and the other half on the day they return. The woman has always paid me through Venmo. The day they returned home, I sent her a request for payment in the app. I also sent her a text telling her that I'd sent the request for payment. She replied with a text, thanking me for *taking such good care of our four leggeds!!! I hope Billie and Cleaver were good! They're both such lovers!!"*

Indeed, they are lovers. If only they weren't such lovers of jumping, licking, sitting on top of me, pulling decorations off Christmas trees, and running away.

I reply, *They are very sweet!* and wish her happy holidays. I check my Venmo app and email several times during the next few hours, looking for a message that I have money waiting for me. But no payment alert arrives.

Thirty hours later, I send a reminder of the request for payment through Venmo, as well as another text to the woman stating that I've sent the second request for payment. She still doesn't pay me. I wait until the next morning and then send her another text.

Me: *If you'd prefer not to pay my balance due through Venmo, I can meet you somewhere in town to collect the cash. Please let me know which you prefer. Thanks* [prayer hands emoji]

Her: *Sorry I've been super busy today. I'm on a conference call now! I'll Venmo your payment this evening or first thing tomorrow morning!!!*

The woman loves her exclamation points. But she still doesn't send the payment.

■ ■ ■

Shortly before noon the next day—after giving her the courtesy of waiting until first thing tomorrow morning has passed—I send another text message: *Is there a reason you're not paying me? Since it only takes about 30 seconds to do a Venmo transaction, I am wondering what's going on. Please explain.*

She does not explain but sends the payment later that day.

■ ■ ■

My calendar shows that I'm scheduled to stay with Billie and Cleaver (and the poultry) again, in about six weeks.

I cancel that gig. With a text message.

And then, with a burst of clarity and glee, I cancel *all* my upcoming critter sitter gigs.

CHAPTER TWENTY-FOUR

In The End

I quit my job as a critter sitter, for many reasons:

1. Shoulder and neck injuries from leash pulling and ball throwing.
2. Mild allergic reactions to some of the dogs: sinus congestion, sneezing, and shortness of breath.
3. Sleep deprivation.
4. More podcast clients after COVID-19 vaccinations and news fatigue prompted public gatherings to resume.
5. The increasing challenges of doing work for my podcast clients while taking care of other people's pets.
6. Stress associated with the fifteen pounds I'd gained from anxiety-related eating: My clothes were too tight, so I was constantly mad at myself. And I didn't feel energetic and healthy.

7. Curmudgeonly thoughts. I felt less tolerance for the bad behavior of animals and people.
8. Less physically capable of controlling large, unruly dogs.
9. Less enthusiasm for picking up poop and scrubbing vomit and pee stains out of carpets.
10. Less enthusiasm for the myriad of responsibilities, expected and unexpected, associated with other people's houses, property, and animals.

It took months for me to admit the truth to myself: I didn't like the work anymore.

Dogs may have behaved as badly in the 1990s and early 2000s as they do now. Maybe. But *I* was different then. I had more patience and more physical strength. I can't seem to stay upright anymore when a ninety-pound dog slams into me at a dead run.

I don't, and never have, blamed the dogs for their behavior. The people they live with haven't given them the training, guidance, boundaries, or consistency they need. And so, the dogs run amok.

Some dogs stand on a couch or in front of a window and bark at anything that moves outside. Anything. All. Day. Long. Their people yell and swat and plead, but they don't make rules and enforce them. The dogs run away and won't come back when called. Their people yell "Come!" until they're hoarse. But they never work with the dogs on a long line to reinforce the command.

The quote, attributed to Oprah Winfrey, "You teach people how to treat you" might also apply to dogs: People teach their dogs how to treat them—jumping, barking, not coming, lunging, growling at other dogs. Each time a dog gets away with bad behavior, that bad behavior is reinforced. My daughter taught me that lesson when she was four years old!

One day, while she waited through *yet another* time out session, I asked Devin why she didn't do what I told her to do so she could go play with her friends, instead of sitting in her bedroom. She replied, "Well, you don't *always* make me do it." In that moment, I knew that if I didn't enforce the rules every single time, she would try to get around them every single time. And dogs are the same. If they can get away with doing what they want to do, they will absolutely make that choice.

The older I get, the less I want to be around bad behavior—in people or pets—but I don't want to be a curmudgeon! And so, I must accept what is.

Bozeman has changed.

Montana has changed.

I have changed.

I am no longer a critter sitter. I am an audio producer, a writer, and a musician.

■ ■ ■

I spent the Christmas holiday at a beach house in Southern California with two of my sisters and one sister's husband. Our time together was relaxing and delightful. We watched spectacular orange and purple sunsets. We spotted dolphins, whales, and sea lions. We watched wetsuit-clad surfers wait hours for the perfect wave to roll in, and then ride it for fifteen seconds. We watched other people watching the surfers. We drank good wine and ate good food.

I rode my bike over miles of the asphalt trails that run parallel to the Pacific Coast Highway and along the beaches near the city of Ventura. I watched a myriad of bird species ride wind currents and strut around poking their beaks into the sand, searching for a breakfast of crabs or clams. I walked on the beach, dodging waves and picking up trash. I dragged a chair onto the sand and sat down to marvel at the ever-changing patterns of water and sand and sky.

For a while I couldn't watch a dog playing fetch or walking with someone on the beach without flinching. I also cringed when I saw dogs on TV or in movies. As the days passed, though, my sudden reactions to random dogs became less intense, and finally dissipated. Eventually, I relaxed and got used to my new normal: a life without responsibility for other people's pets. It was the best Christmas, ever.

But not everyone enjoyed the holiday. Back in the snow and ice of winter in Montana, Dana's struggle continued. On Christmas morning, she sent me a text message: *Merry Christmas! Hope you have a nice peaceful day. I, of course, am at the emergency vet for a client!* [tongue-hanging-out-eye-roll emoji, Christmas tree emoji]

Four hours later, I saw her text—because it was Christmas Day and because I WAS AT THE BEACH! I thumbed a properly compassionate reply into my phone. And then I did a happy dance to celebrate my escape from the anxiety, stress, and life-style instability of taking care of other people's pets.

If you enjoyed this book,
please leave a glowing review at
Amazon and/or Goodreads.
Amazon.com
Goodreads.com
Every review is wildly appreciated!

About the Author

Chérie Newman is a writer, musician, audio producer, and editor. For twelve years she worked at Montana Public Radio, where she created hundreds of programs, news stories, and podcasts. She has recorded interviews in studios located in Bozeman, Missoula, Spokane, Billings, Burbank, and Los Angeles, as well as in coat closets, farm fields, libraries, and hotel rooms all across the states of Montana, Idaho, and Washington.

Her articles, profiles, essays, and book reviews have been published online and in print magazines, newspapers, literary journals, and newsletters. She writes blog posts for MagpieAudioProductions.com and cheriewrites.com.

Chérie Newman lives in Bozeman, Montana, when she's not hiking or riding her bike, *Flash*, somewhere else.